Widow-man

Widow-man

A Widower's Story and Journaling Book

Dr. Nyle Kardatzke

All Scripture quotations, unless otherwise indicated, are taken from The Holy Bible, English Standard Version® (ESV®). Copyright © 2001 by Crossway, a publishing ministry of Good News Publishers. Used by permission. All rights reserved. Quotations marked "NIV" are taken from THE HOLY BIBLE, NEW INTERNATIONAL VERSION®, NIV® Copyright © 1973, 1978, 1984, 2011 by Biblica, Inc.® Used by permission. All rights reserved worldwide. The quotation marked "KJV" is taken from the King James Version.

Front and back cover photos by Nyle Kardatzke.

Editorial Services: Karen Roberts, RQuest, LLC

Printed in the United States of America

For permission to use material, contact:

Nyle Kardatzke
Email: thewidowman@gmail.com

Copyright © 2014 by Dr. Nyle Kardatzke
All rights reserved.

ISBN-13: 9781500333256
ISBN-10: 1500333255

Dedication

This book is dedicated to the widow-men who may read it and to the family members and friends who may urge it upon them. When a man loses his wife, he suddenly finds that "better half" is more than a figure of speech. I hope this book will help widow-men and those who care about them meet the challenges of their new lives.

Contents

Foreword

Life is change. Those three little words have come to represent my basic view of our time in this world. Change can be viewed as a wonderful thing, as in the recent birth of my first grandson, or a terrible thing, as in the death of my first wife. How we understand the changes in our lives and how we choose to respond to them can have a profound and defining effect on what our future will be. I think that is especially true when it comes to what we perceive as negative changes in our lives. The death of a spouse is certainly one of those changes.

The death of my wife of nearly 30 years was a defining change in my life. Susie died of melanoma in 2009, and I was left alone as a father of four daughters, two grown, one married, and one still in high school. Losing Suzie felt like being split down the middle. All the roles she played in my life and in the lives of our children were now mine alone to fulfill. Years of memories, intimacy, and experiences that had been shared by two were now locked away in one mind.

Well-meaning people were quick to let me know that they, or someone they knew, had experienced the loss of a loved one and understood what I was going through. I didn't find that helpful; I didn't care. Those people hadn't lost Susie. Oswald Chambers said, "Never make your experience a principle for others, but allow God to be as creative and original with others as He is with you." I think that is good advice. The loss of a spouse is a very personal experience, and while there are commonalities to all loss, no one else feels exactly what you feel or has the memories you have.

Nyle's book gives room for the men using it to form their own answers and not feel compelled to come up with "correct" ones. Correct answers are not as important in grieving as truthful ones.

I have kept personal journals for years, but during the first years of my grief, I all but stopped journaling, primarily because I was processing so many emotions that to put them on paper felt daunting. It seemed easier not to try. This book would have been a perfect resource for me at that time because it encourages the widowed man to answer questions that he may not give himself permission to consciously think about, let alone answer for himself. Nyle's book helps widowed men understand that their personal thoughts and questions about their lives after loss are normal and that other men have been where they are now.

We all know our earthly lives are finite. We've known it all along. So why do we still feel ambushed by widowhood, whether the loss of our spouse was sudden or occurred after a protracted illness? It's because every death leaves uncharted waters for those still alive. We all need help to navigate those places we've never been before. Help can come in all sorts of ways from people who care about us, from our God, or from resources such as this book. For the widow-man, I highly recommend you take advantage of all of them.

Scott McCracken
Carmel, Indiana

Preface

Your wife has died. You are in shock and grief, and you feel many unwanted changes rushing at you. If this brief description sounds anything like you, this book is for you.

Like you, I lost my wife in death. That was three years ago. Since then I have been learning about this strange new world of widowed men. No one knows exactly how we feel; no one else knows the changing feelings we have as the days and weeks pass. But I hope this book will resonate with some of the things you are going through now, and I hope it will be helpful.

This book has been written in a format to encourage you to make notes about this time of grief and the life you have entered without your wife. I strongly believe healing can come in part through writing about your pain, your memories, and your journey through this "valley of the shadow of death." I know, because I have experienced it.

Long before my wife was diagnosed with breast cancer, I had been keeping a diary and a separate journal on my life and hers. When her cancer was discovered and she began heavy treatment, I wrote in my diary and journal more often and with awareness of the cloud that hung over us. Those writings helped me, especially after her death. In them I could relive some of our life together in a way that I couldn't any other way, even by seeing the family pictures we had collected. What I had written over the years helped me understand and appreciate my marriage after it ended with her death.

A month after my wife's death, I started a new diary on my computer when I realized I was passing through very important, new territory. I knew then I was not likely to clearly remember enough of it when my emotions had settled, and I was again absorbed in daily events. That diary had the advantage of being legible (my handwriting isn't as bad as some people snidely suggest), and I could write much faster on the computer. Later I could also quickly search that document for dates and specific topics I knew I had written about. That computer diary has helped me track my progress in my new life as a widowed man.

Each chapter of this book addresses one question or concern common to widowed men. A brief Scripture or other quotation opens each chapter. I share something from my personal experience, and then I raise questions that you may answer in writing. You may choose not to write each time I suggest it, and you may find that some of my chapters don't apply to you. In addition, the order of the chapters may not be in the order most useful to you. So feel free to read what you want to read when you feel like the time is right, skip around, and use what's most helpful. This book is designed for your longhand notes as you interact with it, and my hope is that it will lead you to do further journaling and diary keeping in the future.

A major fact about grief is that everyone's grief is different. The causes of grief vary widely, our emotional makeups are different, and our relationships with our wives differ from person to person. Since we each experience grief differently, your task, as you work through this book, is to examine and come to understand what *you* are going through.

"Going through" is an important concept to recognize about grief. I was once told during a difficult time: "You will *get through* this, but you'll never *get over* it." How true those words are. You will get through this time of shock, grief, and loss, but you will never completely get over the loss of your wife. She was a very big part of your life, more important to you than you may have realized until now, and the life you shared is a permanent part of you.

You will come out the other side of this grief, and it will become a priceless part of your life. Even now you probably understand the grief of others better than before. As you continue to learn and grow and sometimes struggle, you will gain deeper insights into life because of this pain and sadness. You are headed for better days.

I hope through this book that I can be a companion on your journey as you discover the new life into which God is leading you.

"Those who sow in tears shall reap with shouts of joy!" Psalm 126:5

"The Lord is my shepherd. . . . He leads me beside still waters." Psalm 23:1-2

Acknowledgments

I wouldn't have written this book if my wife, Darlene, were living. Her love and wisdom carried me through our 39-year marriage, and her self-discipline helped focus my naturally wandering mind on my work, our marriage, our family, and the churches where we worshipped and worked.

This journaling book came about through the encouragement and example of Dr. Donna Thomas, a "cousin of a cousin" whose sixth book was a journaling book for widows. In promoting her book, Donna learned there was a need for a similar book for widowed men. She encouraged me to write such a book. *Hope for Today and Tomorrow,* her journaling book for women, provided many helpful reminders of what I experienced and learned as a widowed man in my grief journey. This book is patterned after hers. Without her leadership and encouragement, I would not have made this effort.

I am also indebted to my editor, Karen Roberts, who showed me early on how her editing could make my writing clearer and better organized. A sample of her editing emboldened me to continue with the project that Donna Thomas had inspired. Throughout the editing and publishing process, Karen guided the project patiently and with professional skill.

Several widowed men read portions of the manuscript and "test drove" it for authenticity and usefulness. For their thoughtful comments I am indebted to Dr. Vern Norris, Dr. Greg Hale, Charlie Eldridge, Dan Kirklin, David Blair, and Scott McCracken. All of them have traveled into their own widowhood. Their reactions to the book have been not only insightful but also touching and moving. Dan Kirklin, a friend and professional editor, gave me especially strong encouragement and detailed guidance on an early draft of the book, and Dr. Vern Norris tracked down pesky problems that had escaped my notice until late in the editing process.

Enthusiastic encouragement from my children has renewed my energy often. Their loving companionship during our shared loss has sustained me. Their resilience and visible faith are a joy to me.

Following common practice, I acknowledge that I have had plenty of chances to fix all errors of grammar, fact, and logic that you may find here. Errors that remain may be due to my inattention or to some eccentricity that the professionals couldn't talk me out of.

Introduction: Healing through Journaling

In this book I encourage you to get to know yourself and your journey as a widowed man better. As you read and reflect, you will have the opportunity to capture important moments in your life through journaling: keeping a log of some of your experiences, thoughts, and feelings. There are at least two benefits from journaling:

1. When you get your experiences, feelings, and thoughts out on paper, they become clearer and more comprehensible. You can see them, and they no longer simply swirl around in your head and heart.

2. By recording your experiences, thoughts, feelings, and in some cases also your fears and hopes, you create "memory capital" you can draw upon in future months and years. Sometimes you can better understand where you *are* in life by reading about where you *were*.

Perhaps most importantly right now, journaling is a way to help you understand your new self in the new world you have entered. It can become a tool as you build your new life.

Diaries vs. Journals

I have kept diaries most of my life, but I learned only recently the difference between a diary and a journal. A diary is simply a log of the day's events: what happened, who called, and where I had dinner. I keep a small diary at my bedside in which I write every night just before I turn out the light. It's a set of reminders of the day's events. Though it's mostly mundane and trivial, once in a while it helps me pin down exactly when a certain event occurred. Sometimes that's valuable.

A *journal,* in contrast to a diary, is what I had previously called my "narrative diary." It is a more extended kind of diary in which I think on paper about my experiences and the feelings and attitudes that shape my actions. In it I also include accounts of events in my life and in the lives of my friends and family. Sometimes a week or two passes between my entries there.

Don't assume you will remember all of the important things that will happen to you in the coming year. Experiences that seem so vivid today can evaporate in hours. "Memorable" events can be surprisingly easy to forget. For this reason, I encourage you to try keeping both a diary and a journal. You can use this book as your journal and devise on your own a system for keeping a diary.

I have divided the book into three parts to represent somewhat different aspects of the widow-man's journey. Part One deals with things that go on inside your own mind or in your home: grief, loneliness, safety, and some basic chores of life. Part Two broadens into a view of the outside world and the progression to your "new normal." Part Three takes the longer view of financial issues, your children, possible remarriage, and a very long view of the world after you and I have stepped off this stage of life.

A Man's Job

Keeping a journal is a man's job, and it's especially important in a time of crisis. A wise mentor once advised me, "Take notes on trouble." His advice saved my confidence and my judgment several times when I was in the midst of management crises. My notes helped me understand how some difficult situations had evolved.

Journaling has become popular in recent years, especially among women, but this is not "women's work" in a disparaging sense. It is a mental and spiritual discipline for men or women who are in times of crisis. As a widow-man, you are coming through one of your most difficult and disorienting crises.

Think of your journal in relation to the records kept by the early explorers, from Christopher Columbus to Lewis and Clark. Think of Zebulun Pike or think of John Wesley Powell, the one-armed Civil War veteran who explored the Colorado River from Wyoming to the west end of the Grand Canyon in 1869. They kept detailed journals of their explorations for their own future use and for those who would follow. If you make some journaling entries in the book you have in your hands, you are in good, manly company.

You may also think of your journal in relation to ship captains' logs. Even today those who navigate the seas meticulously record the important events of a voyage. Sometimes they sail through storms, sometimes the weather is fair, and sometimes they are becalmed. They note it all.

Now imagine yourself to be an overland explorer or ship's captain, recording what you experience as you continue your great journey in your new life. It's a man's job.

Maybe Journaling Isn't for You

You may be among the men who won't want to write in this book. That's okay. I think some of the experiences and tactics I describe may be useful for you anyway. You may find it interesting just to think about some of the questions I pose; your thoughts can be your "mental journal."

PART ONE

1

Till Death Us Do Part

"My God, my God, why have you forsaken me?"
Psalm 22:1, Matthew 27:46, and Mark 15:34

Question to Consider: How can I live my life without her?

All marriages end in death or divorce. My wife and I knew it, and we talked about our deaths a few times even when we were both healthy. Sometimes we joked about being each other's "first husband" or "first wife," never imagining there might ever be a second spouse for either of us. We didn't think either of us would die soon; we just assumed we would both die in our old age within a year or two of each other, as our parents had. That was before her breast cancer appeared.

But it has happened, sooner than we'd hoped, and she is gone. It seems so sudden. Death, I'm learning, always seems sudden, even if it is expected, even when it has been expected for a long time. Death is different from all other changes: it is so total, and it is irreversible.

I first learned I was "widowed" when I offered to give blood in my wife's honor soon after her funeral. The young man interviewing me as a potential blood donor asked, "Marital status?"

3

I was confused. I looked down at my wedding ring and stammered, "My wife just died."

"Widowed," the young man said, and he checked that box on his chart.

I felt a little dizzy at that moment, and I thought about my new marital status for a long time. Until then, I had been labeled either "single" or "married." A new label had been given to me, and I was not sure how I felt about it.

How do you feel about death now compared to how you felt about it before your wife died? How do you react to being labeled "widowed"?

Your wife's funeral may have seemed like a blur at the time, and you may remember only a few details now. You had to make some decisions in a hurry when your wife died, especially if she died unexpectedly and suddenly. Some of the decisions you made then, while you were confused and at a loss, may unnerve you now.

Now is the time to be kind to yourself. Remind yourself that you were in an unnatural condition: you had lost your "better half" (or maybe your better three-fourths). "Better half" is a good expression, especially now. It says something important about marriage and about losing your wife. You and your wife really were two parts of one living thing: your marriage.

What memories stand out about your wife's death? The time from her death to the funeral? Make a few notes on the funeral, the people who came, and the decisions you made.

C.S. Lewis said that losing your wife isn't like having your appendix out or being hospitalized with pneumonia: you get over those, and they are forgotten. Losing your wife is like having a leg amputated: you don't get over that. It is such a huge change that it can define who you are for a long time, possibly for the rest of your life.

How do you feel about C.S. Lewis's statement? Is C.S. Lewis right? Do you feel your wife's death defines you as strongly as Lewis says?

Statistics show there are nearly twice as many widows as widowed men in the United States, but the difference seems even greater. Widows seem to be much more visible in society than widow-men. I don't know where all these widowed men are. Like me, you likely have entered, by default, the world of widows. The good news is that you will find some things to learn from the women who have sailed the seas you are in.

How is your life as a man without his wife different from that of a widow?

When I first heard myself labeled "widowed," I wondered what to call myself. "Widow" is usually applied to women, but why can't a man be called a widow? "Widower" makes it sound as though I *did* something, like it's my fault. It's not. I didn't cause my wife's death and bring widowhood on myself. "Widowed" is maybe a better term, but of course she didn't do this to me. Death did; it wasn't her choice either.

I like to call myself a "widow-man." Why? Calling myself a widow-man implies that my situation is different from that of a woman who is a widow. And "widow-man" reminds me of "macho man," a hearty, masculine title. I hope it doesn't resemble "girlie man" to you!

Because more has been written for women who have lost their spouses than for men, recovering from loss of a spouse can sometimes seem like "women's work." In other words, the issues are what people expect a woman—but not a man—to have to deal with. Nevertheless, you, a "widow-man" like me, face some of the hardest work of your life, recovering from her death.

How do you wish to go about this man-size job of being a "widow-man"? In what ways is the death of your wife giving you the toughest work of your life?

2

From Mourning to Grief

"Mourn with those who mourn."
Romans 12:15 (NIV)
"You will grieve, but your grief will turn to joy."
John 16:20

Question to Consider: Where has everyone gone?

Scripture tells us to mourn with those who mourn; it does not say to grieve with those who grieve, but I sometimes wish it did. Mourning and grief are not the same. Mourning has a beginning and a distinct end, but grief goes on much longer.

Mourning is made up of rituals and procedures that immediately follow death: preparing the body for burial or cremation, announcing the death and the funeral plans, the funeral or memorial service, sympathy cards, food taken to the home, and flowers sent for the wake and funeral. These and other rituals and procedures are prescribed in various ways in all cultures. They assure survivors that the loved one is remembered, respected, and sent properly to the place of the dead.

7

What parts of your wife's funeral and the related activities were comforting for you? Which parts are you relieved to be done with?

It is a commonplace that those who have lost loved ones receive lots of attention at the time of the death but are soon abandoned by nearly all well-wishers. What follows is often a deafening silence.

Was your wife's funeral soon followed by a deafening silence? How did you feel about that silence?

The rituals of mourning usually end after a few days. Grief, however, goes on much longer than mourning. For some men, grief continues for the rest of their lives, even though it mellows and may become an integral part of those men's identity. A fine man I know lost his wife and later married one of my wife's sisters. They have a very good marriage, but this man continues to grieve over his deceased wife, even while happy in his marriage.

Why is it important to know that grief is a long-term process and not nearly as well defined as the rituals of mourning?

In Eritrea and Ethiopia, mourning rituals are prescribed at intervals of a few weeks, a year, and even seven years. Nothing, however, is prescribed about grief.

What rituals of mourning might seem good to you to observe after one year, five years, or seven years, even though our culture generally doesn't prescribe any standard behavior for mourners after so long? In what way might you still be grieving after seven years?

The Jewish practice of "sitting shiva" is the custom of going to the home of a grieving family, eating from a buffet, but mainly just being there with the family. You might sit silently for thirty minutes or for several hours. You might speak a few words to one or more family members, but this sitting time is not mainly a time to talk. It's a time to express your sympathy by simply being there. I was able to visit the home of a Jewish man whose wife died of breast cancer. It was a solemn but not tearful time when I was there. Above all, it taught me the meaning of "sitting shiva" in my own Christian culture.

After what you have been through and are going through, in what ways do you feel you are now better prepared for "sitting shiva" with members of families who have lost a loved one through death?

3

Alone Again

"I will never leave you nor forsake you."
Joshua 1:5 (NIV)

Question to Consider: Can I learn to live alone, at least for a while?

One of the first things I noticed after my wife died was the silence. Where she once had been, chatting with me or talking on the phone with others, there was only silence. The house suddenly seemed large and hollow. I especially longed to hear her voice. I still do.

This silence is not like the silence when she was away at work or in a meeting. During those times, I knew she would return, and I could feel her presence in my life, even when she was away. I sometimes needed some time alone, just as she did. This new silence is permanent.

What are your main feelings about being alone now compared to how you felt when your wife was simply out of the house for a while? What single words or short phrases express how you feel?

Soon after my wife died, my mind raced back to what my life was like before I met her. I felt alone, like I was back then. Alone again, starting my life over. For me, it wasn't a welcome feeling. I quickly envisioned the times of loneliness and uncertainty l had before I married her. After her death I didn't feel I had the energy or desire to start over.

How is your present circumstance similar to or different from when you were single before? In what ways do you see your life starting over?

When I lost my wife, I found myself alone, not only physically but also emotionally. Some of my friends couldn't fully understand what had happened. Those friends, though loving and generous, seemed uncomfortable around me, as if they didn't know how to react to me and to my wife's death. It caused me to remember how I used to feel and behave around other people who had lost a family member. I see now that I didn't really understand then the way I do now. So I've had to forgive my friends for how they responded or failed to respond, both initially and in the days and months that followed.

Who was "there for you" and who just couldn't be, either physically or emotionally? What have you learned about grief because of how they responded?

You may need a lot of solitude in the first few months after her death. I did. I especially valued solitude at home. I didn't hibernate and avoid all contact with people, but when my social and church events were over, I felt great relief at being surrounded only by my home. Not all grieving widowed men feel this way. Some resolve their grief by travel, social activity, or volunteer work. Their aloneness gives them freedom to do those things.

When does aloneness lead you to value solitude? How often do you need time away from home with other people, or more people to visit with you in your home?

Being alone is not the same as loneliness. Loneliness comes when you *feel* her absence. Loneliness may rush at you when you are alone or with other people. It may seem to overwhelm you at those times. When loneliness comes upon me, I sometimes just wait it out, or I tell myself it's a natural kind of sadness at this point in life. Sometimes I go to see someone for a short visit, usually not even saying that I had felt lonely. Sometimes when I especially miss my wife, I say her name as though I'm talking to her. It feels good just to say her name, and other widow-men have told me they do the same. Loneliness does recede, but my methods may not be yours.

How do you deal with loneliness? Would you say your basic approach is to fight it, run from it, or accept it as normal right now and take steps to come through it?

Men tend to move on more abruptly than women. Maybe we just don't recognize the depth of our emotions. A widow I know said, perhaps bitterly, "Women grieve; men replace." There's some truth to that. At the beginning, a man who has lost his wife to death may find himself with few companions. The need for companionship can become a powerful driver.

What do you think is the best way for you to deal with your loneliness or need for companionship right now?

4

Confusion

"He will make your paths straight."
Proverbs 3:6 (NIV)

Question to Consider: Why am I sometimes confused about simple things?

If you're like me, you may find yourself confused about common things that once were second nature to you. Deciding on a meal plan or how to spend an evening may seem like big challenges. And some of your better personal habits might be changing now, since your wife helped hold you on course before.

Confusion is to be expected while you are recovering from your great loss. You are not losing your mind.

What confusion have you experienced? How do you respond when confusion comes?

Whether you consciously feel it or not, your mind is overloaded after your wife's death. You are faced with many small decisions every day on top of facing those larger decisions in this new environment. Meanwhile your mind is working in the background on your grief, your memories, your wishes, and your regrets. No wonder many small things are more difficult right now.

Just for the record, what might slip through the cracks right now? What smaller things can you intentionally let go of right now in order to focus on larger things?

Widows say they often feel a great loss of identity after their husband's death. This temporary identity crisis may be a bigger problem for women than for men, especially in the case of women who played a supporting role for their husbands.

For men there is a change in identity too, and you may sometimes wonder who you really are without her. You may have functioned independently of your wife in your work and in some of your social life, but you always knew you were part of a couple. Your name and your wife's name were linked, and your friends used both names when they talked of you. Now there is no "and" in your name; it's only you.

How has your identity changed now that your marital status has changed from "married" to "widowed"?

You may wonder how long it will take you to recover from your confusion and identity loss. Obviously the timing varies widely, and it depends on what you mean by recovery. You have already begun to recover if you are reading this book. You are reaching beyond yourself and taking action to recover. But don't expect recovery to mean you will return to your old self in all respects.

You are in what psychologists label a major "change of life." You are taking on a new life and a new self. Expect confusion, and be kind to yourself. This change of life is so much bigger than just returning to normal.

What do you expect will be your "new normal"? What do you hope it will be like?

Much has changed, even if you are still living in the same house surrounded by the things you and your wife enjoyed together. And you feel different now: sometimes more emotional, sometimes uncomprehending. While she was living, you didn't understand married life in the way you do now.

When you sense these changes, it's good to be thankful for your wife and the life you shared. Thank God for her and also for what you are discovering now about what she meant to you.

What truths about your married life can help you now through times of confusion?

You may not *feel* that God is healing you or that a healing process is underway. Instead, you may be facing each day stoically, practically. Your simple, daily routines are part of your recovery. You accept each day's practical tasks and do them. Just "going through the motions" can sometimes be a major undertaking. Be assured, God is with you, even when moments of sadness come.

What daily tasks help orient you to the day and make you thankful, prayerful, or hopeful for the future?

Married couples vary in the intensity of their dependence on each other. My wife and I loved each other for many years, but our professional lives were separate, as were many of our church and social activities. Her independence would have helped her if I had died first. My independence is helping me now that I'm alone.

What is hardest about your new independence? What is most valuable or most important about it? What do you like the least?

5

Emotions

"You won't always feel the way you do now."
C.S. Lewis

Question to Consider: Will I be overcome by my emotions?

Emotions sometimes seem more real than reality itself. In a time of grief and loss, our emotions are deeper and stronger than at any other time. It's not uncommon to feel we may burst into tears or maybe even physically collapse because of these feelings of grief. Emotion is a natural part of grief, and it may overtake us temporarily, but we don't want to lose control of it. We don't want emotion to magnify our grief, and we don't want to upset others.

Mornings, at least for me, are the most emotional time of each day. I've learned not to judge my day by how I feel when I first get up.

What have been some of your most difficult emotional times since she died? How did you come through those times?

C.S. Lewis wrote in *The Screwtape Letters,* "Humans are oscillating creatures." Our feelings rise and fall unpredictably, perhaps sometimes due to little-understood changes in body chemistry. In the first year after my wife's death, my emotions at times overtook me as I continually tried to grasp fully that she was gone. One evening while preparing for bed, I was suddenly struck forcefully by the fact that she really wasn't coming back. The feeling was one of shock; I even felt dizzy. But another time, while driving to church one Sunday morning, I had an unexpected feeling of peace and joy. At that moment I could remember happier times, and I could sense that happier times would return. The moment of shock and the moment of joy told me something true about what I was going through: it was a journey with many emotions.

How would you describe your mood swings? How can you affect them by the things you choose to read, watch on TV, or spend time on?

My wife had two episodes of heavy cancer treatment, each of which lasted many months. During those times, we were not emotional except in a few isolated episodes. Strangely, I found that I was most emotional when we had good news about her condition, not when bad news came. When we learned that her PET scans were clear during her first cancer treatment, I broke down and cried. When we learned that two forms of chemo had failed after the recurrence several years later, we both looked at it as another objective challenge to be met. We were not overtly emotional about bad news, only good news.

How would you describe your emotions since your wife's death? What single words describe your most frequent emotional condition?

I have to admit, there were times when my judgment was impaired by emotions during my early time of grief. More than once my anger over a traffic situation inflamed absurdly. I growled at people in an airport when I was delayed, though I wasn't even inconvenienced. I sometimes caught myself buying things, and I was sometimes almost tearfully euphoric about some small event. I would soon see these reactions were results of my frayed emotions.

How could your emotions lead you into danger or into hurting the feelings of others? What do you want to be especially on guard about when you are feeling emotional?

Emotions can energize us or cripple us. The goal is not to avoid them but to manage them. The joy you feel in moments of positive, forward momentum is an emotion that supports and nourishes that forward momentum. Try to relish that joy whenever it comes, and be patient when it seems to elude you.

What activities give you a sense of joy, purpose, success, or peace?

Not all grief is openly emotional. Some of our grieving goes on quietly without our noticing and then reveals itself in a new feeling of peace. I'm sometimes surprised and pleased to find my life coming together in a new and comfortable way. Grief has been at work behind the scenes.

When have you had unexpected moments of peace? What thoughts come to the surface during those times of peace?

6

Fears

*"Fear stifles our thinking and actions. It creates
indecisiveness that results in stagnation."*
Charles Stanley

Question to Consider: Why do I suddenly fear things I didn't fear before?

I was surprised to find myself fearing things I hadn't feared before or hadn't feared as much before she died. I might have been forewarned if I had known before her death what C.S. Lewis said about his grief: "No one ever told me that grief felt so like fear." (*A Grief Observed*)

When I knew I would be alone in the house for the first time after her death, for example, I was afraid because I didn't know what my emotional reaction might be. I asked my son and his wife to stay in a guest bedroom that night. My fear of being alone in my house subsided, and the next night I was fine.

Within a few days, to my surprise, new fears intruded: running out of money, being sick with no one to care for me, making bad decisions without the benefit of her wisdom, and breaking down and crying in front of people. As with many grief experiences, I simply had to learn how to go through the times when these fears arose. I learned to deny the reality of some fears, and I searched for the actions I could take to deal with others.

What are your new fears, or what fears are now much stronger than before?

A widow friend of mine has told of fearing air travel after her husband's death, and I know other widows fear driving and being in public places surrounded by strangers. Most men don't experience these particular fears. There is enough of the bully in most of us men to make us feel we can "push" past our fears and make things turn out as we want. This bully or bulldog impulse, however, may make us surly with other people if things go wrong at the airport or in traffic or in a line at the store. It's another example of how men are different from women.

If our boldness as men is a survival trait in times of fear or anxiety, how can it be a hazard, especially when our minds are clouded by grief? What risks could you face?

My biggest fear was running out of money. I had retired only a year before my wife died, and when she died my household income dropped. Although I have Social Security income, and my wife and I had some assets plus equity in our house, I didn't have a feel for how my spending would match my income. I worried about many small purchases, feeling that they might be the cause of my financial demise. This fear wasn't entirely unfounded, and it didn't go away quickly. I often prayed for guidance about my finances, and I gradually came to realize that I could keep my spending within bounds and not become destitute.

How can you deal with your new fears?

Even if you don't have fears about your new life, other people do. Your adult children may fear for you even if they have little reason to do so. Friends may fear for you, especially if you expressed natural, open emotion at the time your wife died or at her funeral.

What worked for me was to keep in touch with those people. I didn't ask about their fears; mere contact with them restored their calm. Such actions on your part can help you avoid those solicitous inquiries that are awkward for you and your family.

What can you do to ease the fears of your friends and family members?

Although I am not a Catholic, I am impressed by Pope John Paul II's frequent advice not to fear. The Bible is full of admonitions to deny fear its power over us (e.g., *"Do not fear, for I am with you."* Isaiah 41:10 NIV). These warnings have caused me to wonder why they are so important and so frequent. Surely we are not to be unwise about things that warrant real fear. There must be a deeper meaning in the challenge, "Fear not."

Why do you think the Bible assures us that we should not fear? How do you get through times of reasonable or even unreasonable fear?

7

Anger

"Do not let the sun go down on your anger."
Ephesians 4:26

Question to Consider: Why do I sometimes feel angry?

Anger is one of the common emotions of grief. I have seldom felt angry about my wife's death, and I don't think anger would have been one of her main feelings if I had died first. I don't think this means we had less love for each other; it just doesn't fit us.

Although anger has not been one of my primary emotions about my wife's death, I sometimes feel it when I see couples that appear to be happy together. Then I feel jealousy and a twinge of anger that my wife and I no longer have each other's company.

You might feel anger about your wife's death, your loneliness, and your problems. You might feel anger at God and even anger at her for leaving you. Anger is a natural reaction to loss and tumult in life. If you don't feel angry, that's okay too. It doesn't mean that you loved her less, and it doesn't mean that you aren't hurting. You just aren't reacting that way.

When have you felt angry since your wife died? What made you angry? How long did it last? If you haven't felt angry, why do you think you haven't?

Some men feel angry when well-meaning people say careless things about their loss. "I know just how you feel, because my mother died last year" or "You'll get over it soon enough if you just stop dwelling on the past" are examples. These people mean well, but they are not doing you a favor with their comments.

Why might the well-intended but poor words of others make you angry? What can you do when you are faced with their unhelpful comments?

The anger of grieving persons often is not about any one specific thing. They just feel angry in general. That kind of anger may be somewhat like the false guilt some people feel after the death of a loved one. It's an emotion searching for a reason.

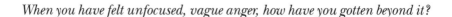

When you have felt unfocused, vague anger, how have you gotten beyond it?

Even if you accept that your wife's death "just happened," it leaves you with her share of the work. That's enough to cause anger from time to time as you shoulder your load and hers too. Although I don't feel angry about the added work, I sometimes feel overwhelmed by it.

How do you feel when you now have to wash the dishes, cook, do laundry, clean the house, or handle invitations and requests for money?

Some widow friends of mine tell me they get angry in grocery stores because they no longer need to plan and cook meals for their husbands. For me, grocery shopping is therapeutic. I enjoy seeing the vast array of foods, and I dream up meals to prepare as I wander the aisles. For other men, grocery shopping is at best an aggravation.

How does grocery shopping affect you? If it's new to you, how does it make you feel and why?

Some widows and men who have lost their wives hate the moment when a restaurant host or hostess asks, "Will there be just one?" or "Are you alone tonight?" One friend has confessed that she boils with anger every time it happens because it points out to everyone within earshot that she is alone. There is a scene in the movie *The Lonely Guy* when Steve Martin goes into a restaurant alone. Everyone stops talking and stares when he tells the maître d' that he is alone. If eating alone in a restaurant is a problem for you, that scene may be therapeutic.

How do you feel about the comment of the host or hostess when seating you alone in a restaurant? Is eating alone in a restaurant an especially lonely time for you or a welcome reprieve from your own cooking or eating alone at home? When does eating alone make you angry?

8

Guilt

"Create in me a clean heart."
Psalm 51:10

Question to Consider: Why do I sometimes feel guilty about my wife's death?

Guilt is another common feeling for those who are grieving. We ask ourselves if we loved our wives enough. We wonder if there was something we could have done to extend their lives or make them more comfortable. Some men wonder if their wives died because of one of their sins, or if that final illness was brought on by tension in their marriage. These thoughts and feelings are often labeled "survivor's guilt."

When survivor's guilt rises up in you, it may seem overwhelming and inescapable. This kind of guilt can be lessened only by truth. This one truth I know: your survival is your last gift to your wife. You survived, and she doesn't have to face life alone without you.

Real guilt is a legitimate warning of something we have done wrong or are continuing to do wrong. It can be seen as God calling us back to the path of right living. Recognizing, admitting, and facing guilt is a sign of a healthy mind. One of the corrupting ideas of our culture is the idea that guilt is always a false and illegitimate feeling, a carryover from outmoded morality. If your guilt is real, you must deal with it before God.

Most guilt feelings after the death of a loved one are false guilt. It is false for two reasons: it arises out of *feelings* of grief, loneliness, and regret, not out of real wrongs. Second, it can't be resolved by actions on your part to put matters right with your wife. You can't go to her and apologize even if you think you need to. You have to find another way to get past the feelings. Some men talk to their deceased wives or write them letters of apology. Some honor her in new ways, such as flowers on her grave or gifts to others in her honor.

When you have felt guilty about your wife since she died, what do you think triggered that guilt? What would you want to say to her about it, and what have you actually done about it?

My wife was very matter-of-fact about her cancer and her shortened life. I followed her lead and dealt with her illness and treatment in the same stoic manner as she did. I sometimes have felt guilty that I wasn't more emotional during her two episodes with breast cancer, but I know she didn't want that—it would have made things harder for her. Many months after her death, I found a diary entry from the year she died in which I noted that I cried very hard in her presence. I was thankful to find that I had shown her my grief that day.

What do you wish you had done differently for your wife near the time of her death? What would she say to you now if you told her your wish?

I was fortunate to be able to care for my wife in both of her episodes of cancer treatment, first in 2003–2004 when the cancer first appeared, and again in 2009–2010 when it returned. I was able to retire in 2009. For the first time in our marriage, we were both at home full time. During that final year, I did most of the cooking, and we shared kitchen cleanup. She did most of the laundry until her strength failed. That year of caregiving has put my mind at ease and kept at bay many feelings of guilt I might have had.

What are some of the things you did right for your wife? How can they help you feel forgiven for things you did wrong?

I received the proceeds from two life insurance policies from my wife. I have had some pangs of guilt about that money, even though I know she would rebuff me for those feelings if she knew I had them. More out of remembrance than guilt, I have been using the proceeds from one of those policies for things closely related to her death and for charitable projects that I know she would have valued.

What things might you do in your wife's honor, even if you are the only one who knows?

9

Forgiveness

"He who is forgiven little, loves little."
Luke 7:47

Question to Consider: How can I forgive and be forgiven?

One of the most preposterous statements from the movies is from the 1970 film *Love Story*. The lead character says, "Being in love means never having to say you're sorry." This statement doesn't even apply to "being in love," let alone real love. In fact, loving another person means often saying you're sorry, unless you are such a perfect person that you never blunder into thoughtless talk or fail to show sympathy and support when you should. Forgiveness is one of the great binding forces in marriage, family life, and love wherever it is found.

Forgiving and being forgiven are among the most healing things that we can do and that can be done for us, perhaps especially in this time of pain and grief. Forgiveness brings wrongs and painful events to a conclusion. It provides a new start and a new life.

To what extent did you and your wife ask for and extend forgiveness? How do you feel about it now that she is gone?

We usually think of forgiveness in relation to some specific, real harm that someone has done. The person who has done the harm may have done it deliberately in a moment of anger or jealousy, or it may be a result of mere thoughtlessness. Forgiveness may come after an apology, and the act of forgiveness may be known to both parties.

Forgiveness after the death of your wife is not of this kind. If there is something for which you need her forgiveness, she can't express forgiveness; nor can you apologize to her directly in person for something you did or failed to do. Forgiveness, however, can happen even though it may not be reciprocal between two parties; it may be a choice by one person, even if no response can come from the other.

What things did you do or fail to do in your marriage that seem to need forgiveness now?

If you think you need forgiveness from your wife, it may be best simply to assume that she forgives you. If you believe she is in heaven, you can assume that she has taken on some traits of God, including forgiveness. In that new life of hers, your wife is wiser and more forgiving than she could have been on earth. Accept her in that new life, and accept her forgiveness.

If there are hurts from her that now make you angry, you can choose to forgive her in your heart and in that way be released from those hurts.

What things did she do or fail to do that are now causing you to feel angry with her, things for which you want to forgive her now?

Forgiving yourself is important. You might think of forgiving yourself as the final step in accepting God's forgiveness and that of your wife. You may need to forgive yourself for failings of yours in your marriage that now make you feel guilty or angry. You may need to forgive yourself for the angry feelings you sometimes still have against your wife even after forgiving her for any wrongs. And you may need to forgive yourself simply for being angry at times about your new situation or at God for letting it happen.

When in the past did you need to accept forgiveness and forgive yourself? For what do you need to forgive yourself now?

Forgiveness is essential to becoming a Christian and to practicing the Christian life. Even outside the Christian life, forgiveness is essential for mental health and emotional freedom. To a Christian, forgiveness begins with God's forgiveness and then extends to seeking and giving forgiveness to others.

What other things, possibly with family and friends, are causing you to feel guilt or anger that need forgiveness?

10

Sleep

"I have promises to keep, and miles to go before I sleep."
Robert Frost, from "On Stopping by Woods on a Snowy Evening"

Question to Consider: How can I sleep enough to get the rest I need?

Sleep is a great healer, but it can be elusive in a time of grief. Some men have trouble falling asleep. Others sleep easily but wake up in the middle of the night. I have had both of these sleep problems. Another is the temptation to sleep a lot, sleeping to escape life and grief. If you have persistent problems sleeping, you may need to see your doctor for help.

My wife had difficulty sleeping in her last few years. I fell asleep almost instantly as I hit the pillow. In the morning, I would ask about her "adventures in the night" to hear about her times of sleeplessness. Now my sleep is more unpredictable, like hers was. When I go to bed, I don't know how well I will sleep.

How well are you sleeping? How concerned are you about your sleep patterns now?

In all the years we were married, my wife insisted on sleeping on the left side of the bed, as seen from the foot of the bed. I complied with her wish and slept on the right hand side. After her death, when I awoke in the night, I sometimes felt that she was there and would reach over to her side of the bed to touch her and find if she was awake.

If you still sleep on the side of the bed you used when she was there, is it a matter of habit, a way to save a memory, or something else?

Your body requires a reasonable amount of sleep, given all you are going through right now. Sleep is part of the healing process. The amount you slept before your wife's death was probably your normal amount for that time in life, but you may not return to it for a while. Be patient; don't try to force things.

Men tend to be problem solvers and want to *do* something. But sometimes we have to live with a problem and let it take its course. Sleep may be one of those problems. If loss of sleep is persistent, however, your doctor can prescribe something to get you through this sleepless phase, and you will later begin to sleep more naturally.

Make notes here about the amount of sleep you need at night and the amount you need in a daytime nap, if you are a nap-taker. How much sleep are you actually getting now? Who can you talk with about this matter?

If you are a praying man, bedtime prayers may help you as well as the people and situations you pray for. Sometimes I have prayed myself to sleep, and I think God accepts that kind of prayer as well as those offered in full consciousness.

What bedtime routines help you to sleep?

11

Starting Your Day

"Oh! How I hate to get up in the morning!"
Irving Berlin

Question to Consider: How can I start my days alone?

Starting the day is a chore for many men and women after the loss of a spouse. When you awaken in the morning after a night in bed, you may feel shaken when you remember that you are alone. It may take some practice to discover the best way to get yourself out of bed, especially if your wife usually awakened before you.

For now, just getting up can be a problem. I sometimes pray before getting out of bed, asking God to guide me and shape my day. That little prayer of humility and dependence on God is sometimes all I can manage. I have found that he does answer that prayer and he makes my day more effective than it would have been. I give him thanks each morning for the previous day, the life God has given me, and the sleep I had in the night, even if it was imperfect.

What helps you get you out of bed in the morning? What is the most pleasant part of your morning routine—coffee, reading the paper, checking email, reading your Bible or some other book, prayer, writing, or a quick shower?

If you typically ate breakfast with your wife, you may find it hard to eat breakfast alone. Since my wife left home early, I usually fixed yogurt and fruit for her to take to work with her, and I ate a fried egg on toast while leaning over the kitchen sink. Since she died, I have continued my own breakfast routine at home, usually eating after 9 a.m. these days.

If breakfast is a problem for you now, one solution may be to find something nourishing you can eat quickly when you are ready to eat, such as a granola or protein bar with coffee or orange juice. If you are a bigger breakfast eater and can cook, it is a good idea to continue to have your oatmeal, pancakes, or bacon and eggs and start your day strong. Many men choose to eat breakfast out, even if they are not widow-men. If doing so gets you up and out of the house in a better mood, do it.

What breakfast foods do you most enjoy, and how can you best enjoy them now?

Healthy morning routines are important. Even a little exercise in the morning can help your day go better. Walking is an ideal exercise, especially if you do nothing else..

If you don't already exercise in the morning, what change in your morning routine might allow time for exercise and get your day off to a better start?

Personal care is important in the mornings even when you don't feel like it. I shave at least every other day, and that makes me feel fit and presentable. Don't let yourself "go to seed." You will notice it, and so will others. The intentional practice of morning personal care routines will help you start your day well.

What do you have to do to feel that your day has started properly?

As part of my morning routine, I take time to pray, read a chapter in the Bible, and write in my journal while I have my first cup of coffee. I don't write in my journal every day, but I do it often enough to follow some of the important threads of my life: my children and grandchildren, other family members, crises in the church and the nation, and memories of my wife.

How do you think you might use this journaling book in your morning routines? Will another time of day work better?

Morning Bible reading can strengthen you and prepare you for the day ahead. Find an amount of reading that is natural and helpful for you. Not all of it will seem meaningful; just keep reading and watching for gems that you will uncover.

What pattern of reading in the morning might serve you well now? Will you read the Bible or something else?

12

Cooking

"He said, 'Throw your net on the right side of the boat and you will find some.' . . . When they did, they were unable to haul the net in because of the large number of fish. When they landed, they saw a fire of burning coals there with fish on it, and some bread. Jesus said to them, 'Bring some of the fish you have just caught.' . . . Jesus . . . took the bread and gave it to them, and did the same with the fish."
John 21:6, 9, 10, 12-13 (NIV)

Question to Consider: What will I cook for dinner?

If Jesus was willing to cook fish for his disciples, we widow-men are in good company if we do some cooking too.

During our marriage, there were periods when I did more cooking than my wife did even though she was a good cook. I enjoyed that task, and I was reasonably good at it. One evening during my wife's final year of life, as I was cooking dinner and she was at the kitchen table visiting with me, I said, "Do you know that I pray the prayer of the Pharisee?"

She was puzzled, so I reminded her of the parable of the tax collector and the Pharisee in the temple. The tax collector beat his chest and prayed for God's forgiveness. The Pharisee prayed by thanking God he was not like other men. I said to my wife, "I also pray nearly the same prayer: 'Thank you, Lord, that I am not like other men. *I can cook!*'"

We both laughed, and I have often been thankful that I can cook, especially now that she's gone. I cook most of my meals, and I like the independence and economy my cooking provides. I make judicious use of some packaged foods to speed things up, and I eat out when I must.

Do you know how to cook, and do you like to do it? If cooking isn't an established skill of yours, how would you get started?

If you haven't cooked much in the past, I encourage you to develop your skills. Cooking can be gratifying, and it gives you a degree of independence you won't have if you must eat out all the time. Eating out is expensive, and it can become a chore. Your home-cooked meals can be healthier than restaurant food: perhaps cleaner and more varied, and you can control the fat, carbs, salt, and sugar.

I strongly recommend the Internet as a source of good cooking ideas. Often I will think of a kind of dish or a specific meat I would like to cook. I just enter the name of the food and add "recipes" and I get more ideas than I will be able to use in a lifetime. Most of these online recipes work well, and you can select one at the level of complexity you want; I usually go for fast and simple.

How would you rate your cooking ability? What about your willingness to cook? What makes cooking enjoyable and gratifying?

Even if you did a lot of cooking before, as I did, you now confront the task of cooking by yourself and for yourself. When I became a widow-man, I became weary of hearing widows say, "It's hard to cook for just one." I was unsympathetic, thinking to myself: "Okay! Cook for four, eat that twice, and freeze two meals for future use! How hard is that?" I was in my third year of widowhood before I felt an emotional burden in cooking for myself. It became harder for me to think of my next meal and to start work on it. I knew *how* to do it, but I didn't feel like *doing* it. Then I began to understand the widows' lament. It's not the physical work of cooking for one; it's the emotional effort of cooking when there is no one else to cook for.

What can you do to overcome the lack of emotional momentum you need for cooking?

I like leftovers, and so did my wife. Leftovers are fast, "free," and sometimes better than the first time they were served. When my wife and I sat down to a delicious dinner of leftovers, I often gave thanks that we both liked leftovers and she would say, "Amen." Those were beautiful moments.

What are your favorite leftovers? How do you supplement them with something new if they need it?

A widow friend was puzzled by her husband's toolbox and soon pitched out all of the tools whose purpose she didn't understand. She was able to focus on relatively few tools for the jobs she knew she could handle. For many men, learning to cook may be the equivalent of that widow's home repairs. Like her, you may find things in your kitchen that you don't know how to use. You may do well to store some of them for the time being or get rid of them if you are sure you will *never* know what they may be for.

What foods can you cook most reliably with the tools you have handy and know how to use? What pattern for meal preparation would you like to establish, given your time, skill level, and appetite?

It's often said, "The shortest way to a man's heart is through his stomach." One of the wiles of women is their skill at cooking, and they can be persuasive that way. I almost always feel better if I cook for company, and I have pleased one or two lady friends by cooking dinner for them. The old adage can work both ways.

Who can you prepare a meal for in your home? What new menus might you try for company?

My companion at mealtime is usually the television. Hearing the news as I cook somehow simulates the presence of another person, so I nearly always check the news or the weather while eating. If the news is jarring or boring, I sometimes talk back to it. Some mealtimes I just watch a portion of a movie.

What mealtime entertainment might help enhance your cooking and eating?

13

Laundry

"Marriage is about the most expensive way for the
average man to get laundry done."
Burt Reynolds

Question to Consider: Now what was it my wife said about mixing colors in the wash?

I had nearly forgotten the important topic of laundry until a friend told me about her widowed father's struggles with his laundry. The same woman said she prefers to do all the laundry for herself and her husband, but she lets him wash his own underwear, socks, and towels: he's not likely to damage those.

If there was ever a really serious conflict in our marriage, it probably was over laundry. My wife had very precise routines to govern clothes washing. I called it "scientific laundry," and to this day I can't tell you all the elements that went into it. The most scientific procedures were applied to her clothing, not mine, so I have very little idea what was involved. What I do know is I could never interfere! Like my friend's husband, I "wandered off the reservation" only at my peril. There were times when I wondered if laundry crises would become a serious threat to our marriage.

Who did the laundry when your wife was alive? What did she wash and what did she allow you to wash? When did you get into trouble for being too helpful or meddling with her laundry?

My friend and her sisters helped their father by giving him tips on laundry and buying him no-iron clothing. They didn't want him to stray into the technical field of ironing clothes. For my part, I'm reasonably good at ironing, and I usually find it therapeutic. It's clean, quiet, indoor work, and if all goes well, wrinkled clothes come in one side and smooth ones go out the other.

What aspects of "laundry science" do you now find especially intimidating? Which of your wife's rules have you found helpful?

I'm still pretty unscientific about laundry, but I have experimented with bleach. It's wonderful stuff! When I found that it would brighten some of my white things, I started using it regularly. I have bombarded underwear, towels, and sheets with chemical warfare. Those successes have led me to use high concentrations of bleach on my kitchen sinks, badly stained old Tupperware measuring cups, and even on my kitchen counters. (Caution! I'm not telling you to try this at home! Please do a little research before trying it on modern countertops. Mine are not modern.)

What new innovations in laundry have you tried or are you secretly plotting to try?

Confession Time: I have violated some of my wife's laundry laws in recent months, and I seem to be slipping into habitual laundry criminality. I have sometimes washed outlandishly mismatched batches of fabric: towels, pillowcases, underwear, socks, and jeans all in the same load. Each little experiment with eclectic laundry has emboldened me to take the next step. I have found that modern colorfast clothing rarely discolors other clothes. Now I am an unrepentant felon where laundry is concerned. I have simplified and expedited my laundry work, and that's worth the shame and guilt my wife might say I should feel.

What violations of your wife's laundry rules have you considered or tried?

A few words of caution from one who learned these things the hard way: don't be as cavalier about your new clothes as I might be suggesting here. Be especially careful to wash new clothes carefully according to the manufacturer's instructions. Use the wash-and-wear cycles for both washing and drying everything if you're not sure what to do. Beware of any colorful clothing whose colors might run. Wash them alone the first few times or maybe forever.

Although I joke about laundry, I know that my wife saved me from many laundry disasters, and she taught me some respect for laundry processes.

What areas of laundry hazard do you plan to respect, even when you are dizzy with power, ready to break new laundry rules every week?

14

Housekeeping

"I hate housework. You make the beds, you wash the dishes,
and six months later you have to start all over again."
Joan Rivers

Question to Consider: How can I manage this house on my own?

In handwritten entries by census takers in the nineteenth century, the occupation of the wife was invariably listed as "keeping house," sometimes just as one word: "housekeeper." It hardly needed to be noted, because very few wives had any other occupation. Women might also help on some outdoor farm work, but it was rare for a man in those days to help inside the house. I'm told that there are still such men today.

You may have shared household work with your wife, but now you are on your own. Even if you did a lot of cooking, as I did, you now have probably already found other aspects of keeping house that are unfamiliar. There are things I do passably well, but dusting and "scientific toilet cleaning" are among my weak points.

What housekeeping tasks do you find manageable or even enjoyable? Which tasks are especially annoying?

A year after my wife died, one of my daughters noticed how little I seemed to be vacuuming, dusting, and doing other basic cleaning. She urged me to find a cleaning person to help, knowing I was unlikely to catch up on everything around my house on my own. I found an excellent cleaning lady in my neighborhood, and her intermittent visits have preserved my cleanliness and my time. In general, I think women have a keener sense of order and cleanliness than men.

What kinds of help should you consider hiring rather than doing the work yourself?

When my wife was alive, we tried to hire cleaning people several times and failed each time. We would work hard the night before the cleaners came to make sure the house was presentable to the very people we had hired to clean it. The cleaning people never cleaned the house to my wife's satisfaction. But we found that whenever we were expecting company, we both became activated by fear of potential shame, and we cleaned the house to a fare-thee-well. We decided we should occasionally invite people over just to force ourselves to tidy up!

Which friends could you invite over for a party, dinner, or TV show to force yourself to see your place as the world might see it and clean it up?

In every marriage, there is a division of labor. One spouse tends to keep the books and watch the budget more than the other. One does more cooking than the other. One is in charge of the laundry, and one maintains the car. Now you must manage it all.

What was the division of labor in your marriage? Who cleaned the house? Who was the bookkeeper, and who was the budget watcher? What new skills do you need now that you are on your own?

A neighbor once told me, "You can't make money by doing another man's job." He had seen me struggling with a yard task that could have been done more easily by a hired worker. His point was that some jobs just need to be hired out. You don't have to do it all.

What do your skills and your preferences suggest about hiring help? If hiring help is not an option, what skills do you need to develop?

15

Safe at Home

"Two are better than one, because they have a good reward for their toil. For if they fall, one will lift up his fellow. But woe to him who is alone when he falls and has not another to lift him up!"

Ecclesiastes 4:9-10

Question to Consider: Is my home a safe place now?

"Safety in numbers" is a common adage that doesn't apply to you as it once did. Your wife was a safety net for you. She probably warned if you drove too fast or didn't notice the traffic slowing ahead of you. Around the house she may have been concerned about dangers that you dismissed casually, like climbing ladders or fixing electrical circuits. Even if you are younger, hazards that were present while your wife was there are now more serious.

You are more vulnerable to home hazards now for three reasons: you are in a state of grief, you are living alone for the first time in years, and you are older than you once were.

What are some possible hazards around your home to pay closer attention to now?

Parents and grandparents take care to "baby-proof" their homes against choking hazards, cleaning chemicals, and open electrical outlets. Older people, too, can turn ordinary things into hazards: leaving stove burners on, climbing on chairs to change light bulbs, tripping while on stairs, overloading electrical circuits, losing track of medicines taken, and forgetting to lock the house.

What steps can you take to "widow-man proof" or "elder-proof" your home? Think about medicines, sharp objects, stairs, fire, floods, windstorms, blizzards, rodents, electrical failures, and burglars.

Five months before my wife died, she abruptly had a home security system installed. She had thought about it for several months and then suddenly decided that it was time. We knew of no active threat to our home, but she felt better to have the alarm system and to have it armed at night. After she died, I found the alarm system reassuring, and I set it every night for several months. The alarm became something my wife did to take care of me after she was gone.

What do you do to ensure the security of your home at night? How would you get help if needed?

A widow friend fell in her unheated garage a few years ago during cold weather. She might have died of hypothermia if she hadn't made a practice of keeping her cell phone with her at all times, even at home. She called for help and was rescued in a matter of minutes.

How would anyone know if you had an injury or a health crisis? How could you call for help?

Some of the best security measures are ancient and time-honored: family, neighbors, and friends. Keep in touch with your kids, friends, and neighbors. Let them know your habits well enough to ask questions if something changes. A widow cousin of mine fell in her kitchen and lay helpless for twenty-six hours, unable to reach her home phone or her cell phone. A neighbor "happened" to come to water her houseplants, thinking she was out of town, and that neighbor saved her life.

Who are the "lifeline" people in your life who may save you from misery or death? How will they know if you are in trouble?

16

Memory and Memories

"Remember your Creator in the days of your youth, before the days of trouble come and the years approach when you will say, 'I find no pleasure in them.'"
Ecclesiastes 12:1 (NIV)

Question to Consider: Am I losing my memory and my precious memories?

Our memories in many ways are the storehouse of who we are. We have practical issues of memory: our ability to remember names, appointments, and where we have left things. There are also memories that we want to keep: mental pictures of scenes we shared with our wives when they were here. Memory and memories make up much of who we are.

Forgetfulness comes with the confusion we widow-men feel. It's hard to remember what we said to each person recently, and we might forget appointments. We may forget where we put something in the living room or kitchen. I often spend time looking for things that I have lost due to forgetfulness.

What problems do you have remembering the things you want to remember and the things you need to do? (If you have no problems, just smile, draw a smiley face, and skip this space.)

In the first few months of my widowhood, I sometimes wondered if I was becoming senile. Was it the onset of Alzheimer's, I wondered? But then I realized I was experiencing shock due to my wife's death, not dementia or Alzheimer's.

If you are an "older man," maybe over sixty, memory losses may worry you a lot. When you forget something, consider that your mind is working hard behind the scenes, and it may neglect to remind you to do even some basic things. Remembering to do simple tasks may require conscious thought for a while.

When you have experienced memory lapses since your wife's death, how did you interpret them? Do you think they were due to her death, your "old age," lack of sleep, or something else?

When your wife died, you *did* lose part of your memory: the part that she always took care of. She reminded you of names, meetings, birthdays, and how to tuck in your shirt. You lost a large part of your sentimental memory bank as well. I often wish I could share a memory with my wife; she is the only other person who might remember and care about some events.

You can enjoy some of those sentimental memories just by thinking about them, and you can store them to remember again by writing them down. Thoughts and memories, even valuable ones, are transient and disappear quickly if not written down.

What are some of your most valued memories? How do they define the person you are?

I take lots of notes and make lists to make up for my wife's reminders. These lists help keep me on track as I go through the day, and they remind me of what I have accomplished when I feel I have done nothing. Because I like lists, sometimes I even add something to a list *after* I have done it, just for the satisfaction of crossing it off the list.

What are your new tasks now? What system would help you measure your days and make them useful?

I not only forget some important things, I also tend to avoid some of them. I tend to avoid financial matters, home maintenance, lawn upkeep, and car repairs. Avoidance can be as risky as forgetting.

What things seem more emotional and frightening than before? Do you try to avoid them? How do you overcome your avoidance tendency?

17

Permission to Change

*"The more decisions that you are forced to make alone, the
more you are aware of your freedom to choose."*
Thornton Wilder

Question to Consider: Why do I feel my wife's presence when I am
about to change something?

My wife and I slept in a king-size bed for the last seventeen years of
her life. After her death, I continued to sleep in that massive bed, but
always on my side, not hers. It was a comfortable bed, but I found I was
swimming all over it at night, and it was hard to make such a large bed
by myself, especially after washing the sheets, when the bed had to be
made from scratch. Changing the sheets seemed to be more work than
it was worth for me alone.

About four months after my wife died, I looked at that king-size
bed one morning, and for the first time it occurred to me that I didn't
have to keep using it. I could use one of the other beds. I winced at the
thought, wondering what my wife would say if she came home and saw
that I had changed things without her permission. It took me half a
minute to realize she wouldn't be coming back to catch me disturbing
our bed. Emotionally I didn't feel that I should be making a change
without her permission even though mentally I knew that it was okay.

I went ahead that day with a major bed-moving operation that ultimately led me to the twin-size bed that now suits me best.

How have you overcome the inertia of needing permission before changing something in your house or in your life? What change was that? What else may need to change?

Several other times I have wanted to make a change in the house or in my schedule and have felt I had her permission to do so. Fortunately my wife was quite practical, so it's easy for me to picture her approving and endorsing some of the changes I have made. But there are still things I leave as they were, out of respect for the space she still occupies in my psyche and for my own emotional pleasure. She liked things this way, and I can still enjoy them for that reason.

What do you keep in place simply because you and your wife liked it that way? When have you felt liberated by making a change that you and your wife disagreed about but that you are now free to change?

Many other widow-men besides me probably need to feel their wives' permission to make changes, especially in the first few weeks or months. Of course we know that it is we ourselves who must grant the permission, but we are more comfortable with those decisions when we feel our wives invisibly agreeing, maybe smiling and nodding from where they are. My wife's name was Darlene, so I sometimes ask myself, "WWDD"? ("What would Darlene do?") I often receive assurance about an action by asking that question, and I have been diverted from disasters in the same way.

How might it help your peace of mind to sometimes ask, "What would she do?" How would doing so intentionally increase your pleasure in some daily routines? In what areas of life management would that question be good for you to ask so you could draw upon your wife's wisdom?

Small household changes are one thing; new relationships, especially with women, are another. Some men never feel they have permission to see other women, to say nothing of remarrying. Others make this transition easily. Still others can do so because their wife told them she wanted them to remarry.

In what areas of your life have you felt inhibited about making changes, feeling that your wife didn't want you to do so? What changes have you made, and which ones may be ahead?

18

New Decisions

"The LORD gave Solomon wisdom, just as he had promised him."
1 Kings 5:12 (NIV)

Question to Consider: How can I make good decisions?

Grief counselors recommend delaying major decisions while you are still in the throes of grief. A year of recovery is often advised for matters that can wait. But there are some decisions and actions that you need to take soon after her death. Many of these are financial decisions that require promptness: taking her name off credit cards and bank accounts, collecting life insurance money, and paying funeral bills. If her body was cremated, you need to collect her ashes and either scatter them according to her wishes or store them until you can.

Making some of those decisions gave me a feeling of closure and assurance; others produced anxiety. Some of them made me feel I was burying her over and over. I was unsettled to learn how my income would drop without my wife's disability income and her Social Security payments. One of the toughest decisions I had to make was what to do about this significant change of income.

How do you feel about the financial and legal facts that you have learned since your wife's death? Which new things were most surprising?

Some of your big decisions are behind you: details about her funeral service, her burial, her casket, or the disposal of her ashes if her body was cremated. Other decisions are ahead: how to change your will, changes in your investments, keeping or selling your house and her car, what to do with her clothing and other belongings, and whether to maintain all of the friendships that the two of you shared. Take your time on these decisions. As much as possible, maintain the status quo for a time. Changes will come soon enough, and it will be good if you have established a stable frame of reference before you make the bigger decisions.

Which decisions must you make in the next month, whether you wish to do so or not? Which decisions do you think you can delay? Think of decisions that would be irrevocable or costly in money and emotions if you were to make an error through a snap decision.

My wife and I made all of our important decisions jointly, and we often enjoyed sharing small decisions. Like me, you may have lost your wisest and most knowledgeable advisor. Chances are she complemented your decision-making patterns by questioning them and adding her perspective. Now you need to develop a new decision-making process to use in her absence.

How did you and your wife make decisions? How will you make up for not having her thoughts on the decisions you now face?

My wife made some decisions better than I could. I am especially vulnerable in the area of home decorating. I shudder to think what our house would look like today if I had been in charge of decorating it. That's a vulnerable area for me. She also excelled in detailed cleaning.

In what areas of decision making are you especially vulnerable now? How will you handle those decisions now?

In your investments, as well as in more personal decisions, your tolerance for risk probably is lower now since you don't have the emotional security of your wife's presence, and you don't have the financial security of her income. For these decisions, a wise friend, family member, or financial specialist can help you allocate your investments in keeping with your age, health, and responsibilities.

Learning to make good decisions on your own is hard work. Especially now, it will be wise to write down the arguments for and against your major decisions. Getting them out of your mind and onto paper will help you see the consequences of your choices and will take some of the emotion out of them.

How do you make decisions? Do you analyze things at great length or act quickly to economize on time? How do you think you can improve your decision making? Who can you talk with about your big decisions?

19

Her Clothing, Her Things

"And why do you worry about clothes? See how the flowers of the field grow. They do not labor or spin. Yet I tell you that not even Solomon in all his splendor was dressed like one of these."
Matthew 6:28-29 (NIV)

Question to Consider: What should I do with my wife's clothing, jewelry, books, and other possessions?

I believe our wives are now clothed in splendor that Solomon could not have imagined, but we still have their earthly clothing here, and we must deal with it sooner or later. You now have a task that nothing has prepared you for: what to do with your wife's many belongings, including her clothing.

There are no rules for dealing with her clothing, books, jewelry, and other possessions.

You must consult your feelings and your habits as you begin this work. Don't be in a hurry. If you are a very tidy person and you need closure soon, you may decide to act faster than a man who has storage space and is comfortable with so many reminders of his wife.

Since there are no rules for dealing with her belongings, what "rules" might you create to help you decide what to do with her things?

When my wife died, I thought it would be weird if I still had her clothes in the house a year later, as though I kept them out of some morbid fixation. I was wrong about that, and I still have some of her clothes now, three years later. I did give away many armloads of clothing in the first few months, and in the very cold winter of 2011, I gave most of her coats to African refugees. My one regret is giving away a coat that she wore on camping trips. I didn't realize until too late that she appears in many camping pictures in that coat. But the coat kept someone warm, and that meant more.

Which of your wife's possessions have special sentimental value to you? How can you respect your memories and your emotions in deciding what to do with them?

A friend recommended that I not donate any of my wife's intimate apparel but discard those things instead. The advice seemed wise. I have also discarded other personal things like her cosmetics. I take digital pictures of the things I decide to give away or discard, except for intimate things. In this way, if I must, I can still see the discarded or donated objects without having them in the house.

What procedure can you follow for storing, donating, or discarding some of your wife's belongings? Which things will be easiest to discard or give away? Where do you want to begin?

Know yourself. Does it help to keep some things and feel she is still there? Or do you need a clean break? Consider storing some things away from the house if you are crowded or if you just need separation from her belongings. Consider your children and friends. What do they need to see in your home to assure them of your love for your wife?

I have kept pictures of my wife on display throughout the house. Some are formal portraits of us with our children when they were younger, some are snapshots taped to cabinets in the kitchen or the refrigerator. I have gradually put away a few pictures of her, but many will remain in view.

When my children visit, they still see some of my wife's clothes in a couple of closets, but they rarely comment on them. My children may feel some comfort in seeing their mother's clothes, and I have no need to discard them yet.

What can you do to avoid the grief of seeing her things everywhere and yet protect yourself from the regret of getting rid of them too soon? What can you do to respect the feelings of your children and your wife's family?

From time to time I find things that I think are especially appropriate for one of our children to have. I explain the significance of each object when I give it, sometimes writing about its history. I sometimes give things related to my own life as well as my wife's, since I don't expect to be here forever. A few times I have given things to my wife's two sisters, but my children generally have priority. I haven't yet identified pieces of furniture that might be keepsakes for my children; that process needs to be on my list.

What things would be especially good for you to give to your children now? What things do you think it would be best for them to receive after you die? What things do you want to be able to see for as long as you live?

PART TWO

20

Returning to Your World

"There is nothing like returning to a place that remains unchanged
to find the ways in which you yourself have altered."
Nelson Mandela

Question to Consider: Will I ever return to normal?

Your wife's death, the funeral, visitors, and necessary follow-up activities probably kept you away from many of your former, usual activities for a while. You came through some traumatic times. You experienced many changes, not all of them yet entirely clear to you. Your life had to go on, but it seemed strange, very strange, at first. You probably wondered more than once when or if your life would return to "normal."

My son said it was eerie to return to his hospital work after his mother's funeral. People weren't sure how to react to him at first. Soon "business as usual" took over, and everyone was relieved.

If you are currently employed, what was it like to return to work after your wife's death and funeral? How did you handle people's questions? If you are retired, what familiar places at first seemed strange?

Returning to church after my wife's memorial service seemed like a big hurdle to me. As retirees, church was one of the main places we met people. Her memorial service was on a Saturday, and I didn't go to church the next day or for a few weeks. When I did return to church, it was easier than I expected. I don't remember where I sat or with whom, only that it was easy and comforting to be there again.

What was it like to return to church and other gathering places or social events the two of you attended regularly? How long did you wait?

When we had free time, my wife and I were homebodies. Our professional lives kept us so busy we didn't have time or inclination to socialize much with other couples. Our social life was mainly through our families, church, and work.

Some married couples are socially involved with other couples, and that sometimes changes painfully when one spouse dies. I know several widows who have been hurt and angry when the married couples they had previously enjoyed no longer invited them for dinner or travel. Perhaps a widow or a widow-man seems like a threat to the marriages of the other couples, or maybe the problem is merely having the right number of place settings at the table.

What do you miss about the social life you and your wife shared? What couples still matter the most to you now? Why?

By now you probably realize there's no going back to your life as it was when your wife was still alive. You're in a new life now, on a different journey. Those places that now feel awkward or difficult to visit again will take on a different appearance after a time. This part of your life is like going through a passageway: you will come out the other side.

How will you recognize that "other side" when you get there? Write down what you think it will be like when you have fully entered your new world.

21

The First Year

Question to Consider: Why is this first year so important?

In the first year after my wife's death, I was in a world of unreality. Each day seemed like a new event, even though my surroundings hadn't changed. Looking back, I can see that I was in something like a state of shock, just carefully going through the necessary activities but feeling oddly outside myself, an "out-of-body" experience. I had to repeatedly learn that she really wasn't coming back.

My diaries for that year show that I thought of my wife almost constantly. I made journal entries about my feelings during that first year and about the years of our courtship and marriage. I examined in detail everything I could remember about her and about our life together. When she had been gone three months, I wrote that this had been a long time, but now three *years* seems short.

If you have been a widow-man more than a year, what is most memorable about that year? If you are newly widowed, what are your plans for the first year?

My journals from that first year tell me I maintained some of my old routines, thinking subconsciously that those routines, as rituals, might bring my wife back. I knew this was impossible, but the rituals seemed to make the parting easier.

What routines of yours now seem like rituals to retain memories of your wife, or the feel of her presence?

The first year after the death of a loved one is always a special one. Books on grief always give much attention to the emotional impact of reminders of the loved one as each season, each birthday or anniversary, each holiday comes and goes in that year. In addition to the emotional impact, that first year is a time of learning how to manage activities and relationships without the one who has died.

Besides holidays, birthdays, and anniversaries, what milestones during the first year might be emotional times for you? What activities require a new approach? If you have been widowed more than a year, what have you learned that can be helpful for subsequent years?

When I approached the end of the first year, I felt I had accomplished something important by completing that year, and yet I felt some regret in continually moving farther away from when she was alive. I also expected an unrealistically clear turning point after that first year.

In what ways do you expect all future years to be different from the first?

In one of our last conversations, my wife advised me not to make any big decisions for a year after her death. I knew this advice made sense; she was thinking more clearly than I could about her death. When she died a week later, the enormity of her death hit me. I was thankful for her advice.

What advice, if any, did your wife give you about how you should live after her death? What agreements did you make with her (or now wish you had) about your life if she died before you?

All of the milestones of the first year are potentially laden with emotions. The changing seasons, holidays, birthdays, and anniversaries often are difficult as they come around for the first time without your wife. Widows warned me about them, but they were still difficult to navigate.

What vows have you made or wish to make now about how you will live this year? What are the mottos or watchwords that will guide you?

22

Laughter

*"I'll never smile again until I smile at you. I'll never
laugh again, what good would it do?"*
Frank Sinatra

Question to Consider: When can I laugh again?

I seldom look to "Saint" Sinatra for inspiration, but the lines from that song he crooned capture the feeling of many grieving widow-men. For me it has sometimes seemed like a song sung to my lost wife, looking forward to seeing her again in heaven, where I can truly laugh again with her.

Laughter may seem like an odd topic in a book for men who have lost their wives, but it can be a real issue. Even smiling can sometimes feel like using unfamiliar muscles. But smiling and laughing, when they come, are truly gifts that contribute to healing.

As I traveled further into widowhood, I caught myself laughing about some of the things my wife and I used to laugh about. These often were antics of our grandchildren or funny turns of phrase that one of us happened upon accidentally while talking to each other. In her last year of life, my wife said some very funny things that made me laugh and laugh. At the time, I sensed these were especially precious moments because we both knew her health condition was perilous.

Do you sometimes feel you will never really laugh again? When you smile now, does it feel like you are using muscles that have been dormant a long time? How do you feel when something suddenly makes you laugh?

I have never felt guilty when a joke or a line in a movie makes me laugh, but some widow-men tell me they do, at least at the beginning. They feel they would be betraying their lost wife if they reentered the world of laughter. Please be assured, you haven't ceased grieving over your wife if something funny makes you laugh. You are still grieving, and laughter is part of the healing process. Laughter can feel good when it returns, even perhaps if only for a few fleeting moments at first.

What is there about laughter now that makes it difficult for you? If you have laughed and later felt guilty about it, thinking it was maybe too soon, what do you think is holding you back or causing you to feel guilty about laughter now?

You are walking through the valley of the shadow of death, but I hope you know this path will take you to wisdom and joy. Joy is not the same as simple happiness, giddiness, or humor. It is a more profound kind of happiness that comes from a deeper experience of life. It comes with understanding and wisdom. You are learning things about life and death that not all men experience. You are unique, and you experience life and death in your own way.

What do you think joy will be like when you find it? What might help it return?

I can't tell you how to enjoy laughing again or laughing more if it has already returned. But I can tell you a couple of things that have worked for me. One is to see an old movie that my wife and I used to enjoy and laugh about. There are lines from a couple of old movies that she and I could readily recite when absurd things cropped up in our lives, so I have revisited those movies and enjoyed new smiles and chuckles, if not loud outbursts of laughing.

Sometimes it helps to see absurd TV shows like "America's Funniest Home Videos." Sometimes those are actually funny. Good books bring chuckles too. If there is a book you once enjoyed for its humor, it might make good reading when you are ready for a laugh. If you haven't read them, you might get smiles from *The 2,548 Best Things Ever Said* or *The 2,548 Wittiest Things Ever Said*, both by Robert Byrne. But don't force yourself; don't make this an artificial project. Wait for the right time.

One of my great sources of laughs in the last year has been an 85-year-old woman from the Sunday school class I teach. She sends an endless stream of email forwards, many of which have me in stitches, and her funnies are clean enough for her to send to many others in our church.

What movies were funniest to you and your wife? What books made both of you laugh? Which of your friends can you count on for funny email forwards that are clean enough to feel good about?

23

Holidays

"We must hold a feast to the LORD."
Exodus 10:9

Question to Consider: How can I get through the holidays when others seem so happy and I'm sad?

When I think of holidays, I think immediately of Thanksgiving and Christmas. My wife died on October 25, so those two holidays were a shock. I didn't intend to immerse myself in open, emotional grief, but I didn't want to pretend that nothing had changed either. They were a challenge that first year.

I wasn't sure how I would react to Thanksgiving, but I knew I needed to decline invitations from my wife's family to join them. My son and his wife joined me for a quiet lunch and afternoon. In the evening, we went to Cracker Barrel for Thanksgiving dinner. Half of the Hoosier nation was there, it seemed, but we had a traditional turkey dinner and felt that we had done justice by Thanksgiving.

What ideas can you think of to make the Thanksgiving holiday special for you? What about your family?

Christmas marked exactly two months after my wife's death. My adult children and four young grandchildren asked if they could all come and stay at my house. I knew I had to decorate the house to some extent rather than broadcast to these young people that I was alone, sad, and in shock. Christmas decorating was a project my wife had always led, so my mind felt like oatmeal and my body seemed leaden.

I could hardly go through the motions of testing the lights, putting them up, and getting the tree from the attic. Thankfully my son and his wife came to help, and the house began to simulate one celebrating Christmas. That year's decorating was far below the standards my wife would have expected, but it was enough to signal to me and to my family that life was going on. The holiday I had dreaded became a step toward the future.

On the third Christmas after my wife's death, I was at the home of one of my daughters. It was a first for her and her family to have a grandparent there, and it was a first for me to have Christmas in the home of one of my children. I now have had four Christmas seasons without my wife, and each has become easier, happier, and more focused on family, friends, and the future.

What parts of your former celebration of Christmas will you retain this year? What changes do you expect to make? Will the holiday be best at your home or somewhere else?

Holidays won't be the same without your wife, but they won't always be an emotional challenge. You may find altogether different ways to celebrate them, maybe at home with some of the same decorations and foods, or maybe in someone else's home or in a restaurant. And locations can change from year to year. Many families make this choice to accommodate the needs of extended families.

Here is what I have learned about celebrating the holidays, especially Thanksgiving and Christmas. Be open to let the holidays begin to shape themselves as you try to find new ways to observe them. Don't overdo it to cover up the loss, but also don't make a big show of *not* feeling like celebrating them. Either choice will only make you and others sad.

If you build a wall of gloom around yourself, people won't want to try to break through that wall. Everyone will lose.

How do you feel about the holidays of the coming year? Which ones will be most emotional for you? How do you want to deal with them? Who might be able to help you?

24

Other Special Days

"Where there is great love, there are always wishes."
Willa Cather

Question to Consider: How can I celebrate other special days?

Behind every special day, there is love. It may be an experience of past love, or it may be a love to be wished for. Even patriotic holidays reflect love: love of country and love for those who have served it well. Thanksgiving and Christmas holidays have their established traditions, and learning how to celebrate other special days now that your wife is gone is an important part of your journey.

Birthdays were more significant for my wife than for me. Her family celebrated them more thoroughly than mine. She delighted in decorating special cakes for our kids, and she gave me thoughtful gifts. I tried to be faithful about birthdays, but I was not as creative as she was. Now I remember her birthday annually, and more. It was November 3, so I think of her when my digital clock shows the time as 11:03.

How did you and your wife celebrate your birthdays? How do you think you would like to observe her birthday in coming years? What about your own birthday?

Our wedding anniversary, in June, was a special day for my wife and me, even if we didn't do something unusual to celebrate it. Sometimes her work or mine prevented a special dinner, but we always found some way to commemorate our wedding day. When we had been married over twenty-five years, we started a list of what had happened on each of our anniversaries. I keep up that record now with short journaling entries.

How did you and your wife celebrate your wedding anniversary? What ideas do you have for celebrating that special day in the coming years?

Valentine's Day may have been an important holiday for you and your wife. My wife and I had the strange practice of giving old Valentines to each other year after year, adding the date for each year we used them. I miss that zany little practice, but it's a treasure to remember. Now I send Valentines to my daughters and my daughter-in-law, and I'll soon send them to my granddaughters when they are a little older. Sometimes I send cards to other female relatives, especially widows. I feel better if I do something about Valentine's Day instead of merely letting it pass by. I think my wife would approve.

You, like many men, may have felt coerced into making a show of romance on Valentine's Day. Don't let that thought bog you down in guilt now; chances are your wife knew how artificial Valentine's Day can be and appreciated your love for her throughout the year more than your Valentine's Day gestures.

What can you do now to plan for the upcoming Valentine's Day? In what ways is your plan different from the Valentine's Day times of your past?

Mother's Day can be an especially tender time for your children, maybe more than for you. Your children knew her all of their lives. I like to send Mother's Day and Father's Day cards to my children and in-law children and others I appreciate for their parenting. I try to remember my wife's siblings; they are grieving her too.

To whom can you send your Valentine's Day cards now? How can you choose to observe Mother's Day?

Memorial Day is a somber, reflective day for some families. My mother's family called it "Decoration Day" when I was a boy. For me it was just a nice, warm day out of school, and the main observance was a parade in our little town, followed by the Indianapolis 500 on the radio.

After my wife died, Memorial Day took on a new meaning. My wife had requested that her body be cremated, so the times and places where my adult children and I took her ashes formed special memories for us. I remember with poignancy the days when we took her ashes to the beautiful places in Colorado that she requested.

What memorial practices might you begin this year in your wife's honor? If your wife's body is in a cemetery, what would you like to do this year there to honor her memory on Memorial Day?

The anniversary of your wife's death probably always will be special to you, one of your most sacred days of the year. If you are like me, you may even observe her "monthiversary" on the date of her death each month.

In my early days as a widow-man, that date, the 25th of each month, hit me like a blow to my chest. As time has passed, the date increasingly became a day when I chose to have a few moments of reflection and thankfulness. Sometimes my children mention it; mostly now, however, we let the day pass without notice.

How do you wish to observe the anniversary of your wife's death this year and in later years?

25

Weekends

"Remember the Sabbath day, to keep it holy."
Exodus 20:8

Question to Consider: How can I make the most of weekends?

Holidays and other special days of the year are a challenge to grieving people. Likewise, weekends can feel like recurring holidays that bring fresh emotional pain or joy. Before I was married, weekends were a greater challenge than the major holidays, since I could readily follow enough of the standard scripts for holidays. Then, weekends were unscripted except for the expectation of getting dates and having fun, neither of which was easy or successful all the time in my days of singleness. I began to see that one great advantage of getting married was I would no longer have the hard work of finding a date and something to do for the weekend.

During my married years, weekends were a welcome reprieve from the pressures of the work week. Early in our married life, my wife and I often ate out on Friday and slept later than usual on Saturday. That was before kids, of course. With the kids, pancakes and bacon was our traditional Saturday breakfast. On some days, the kids and I just let my wife sleep in while we went to McDonald's. Sunday morning was always "church time," and that afternoon became homework time. Those were wonderful weekend times.

What were your favorite weekend activities? How did those change over the years you were married?

Now that I'm a widow-man, weekends are not the same challenge they were when I was in my 20s. I don't feel pressure to get a date, and I often welcome the relative calm I feel on weekends. Nor are weekends like those when my wife was alive, when we were busy doing things together or with our kids. Now feelings of loneliness or cabin fever often come on weekends, and I'm relieved when Monday comes around. I'm sure many other widow-men have pangs of loneliness on weekends too.

How do you feel about weekends now? How do they feel compared to your weekdays?

I'm retired now, so weekends aren't very different from the rest of the week except for church activities that occupy my Sunday mornings. If I were holding a job now, I'm sure I would make more productive use of my weekends: grocery shopping, basic cleaning and laundry, home repairs, car upkeep, and correspondence.

If you are employed, what is best about the weekends? What do you need to learn about managing your time on the weekends, whether you are employed or not?

Other people's social lives generally revolve around weekends, so if I want to spend time with them on a weekend, I often have to schedule it several days or even a few weeks in advance. I have to be proactive. If I am not, I face too much time alone, enough that I get tired of my own company.

In your new life, how do you manage to see other busy people on weekends?

The idea of a "Sabbath" time of rest basically means a time unlike the ordinary days. It can mean voluntary isolation from the pressures of daily life, and it possibly might include restrictions that resemble those of Bible times. More likely, a Sabbath rest comes in smaller pieces on weekends and may be a change of pace rather than cessation of activity. For some people it includes exercise, taking a nap, cooking something special, or going out for dinner or a movie. There is wisdom in finding Sabbath times in your week, whether for a whole day, an afternoon, or only for an hour or two made intentionally different from all the others.

What kinds of change of pace do you want on weekends? What do you have to do routinely during the week to make sure weekends include some kind of "Sabbath" time of your design?

26

Finding Help for Your Grief

"Seek, and you will find; knock, and it will be opened to you."
Matthew 7:7

.

Question to Consider: Who can help me with my grief?

Losing your wife is so all-encompassing that it may not be comparable to any other loss except possibly the death of a child. The complete intertwining of your life with another in marriage makes the loss of your wife a distinctly life-shattering, life-changing experience. For this reason, many men find they need both informal and formal help from others in managing their long-lasting grief.

List the names here of other widow-men or widows whom you think might come close to understanding what you are going through. Who else might understand?

My church contacted me about the grief support groups held several times each year through our Stephen Ministry. The groups were conducted on an "as needed" basis, and the next group wasn't scheduled to begin for about five months. While I waited, I learned online about several other places for grief support: other churches, hospice care, and hospitals.

I was the only widow-man in the group of eight I joined; the others were all women, and only one was a widow. Everyone in the group had lost a family member through death, generally siblings or parents. Some had lost loved ones only a week or two earlier; some were grieving deaths from a few month ago. It might have helped me more if there had been another widow-man in the meetings, but I found I still could learn from those experiencing other sources of grief. Perhaps I encouraged the others.

What grief support groups have you heard about or researched online, and how do you feel about being with other grieving persons in a support group? What value might there be in it for you and the others in a group?

As I said in the first chapter of this book, there are far more widows than widow-men. Finding widow-men can be a challenge, and it can be a challenge for them to find you. Having a meaningful conversation with a widow or a divorced woman might be a substitute for talking with other widow-men, since many men don't readily talk about their feelings.

Why might it help you to talk to another widow-man or a widow? What value could there be to you in sharing the grief of one who has lost a parent or a sibling, not a spouse?

In the three years since I was in that grief recovery group, I have seen some of the group members at church. We have never again talked about the experiences that brought us together in grief, but there is always a bond of friendship and understanding when we see each other. Our shared experience in the grief group is part of our journey now. We shared our sorrows when they were fresher than now.

What good might come from sharing your grief with people you don't know now but may see again in other circumstances? What might make you feel like avoiding that kind of conversation?

The husband of a good friend in a distant city died six weeks before my wife died. She and I had known each other for nearly fifty years. After we both lost our spouses, we became our own two-person support group through a constant stream of emails. We reminisced about our spouses' final illnesses, our families, and some of the struggles we felt in our time of grief. When we found a wonderful book of meditations for grieving people, we began to email about the readings every day. Our two-person group was a rare discovery, and we both felt it preserved our mental health during that most difficult time.

List the names of three people with whom you think you could talk freely about what you are experiencing. What form of communication would work best for you: face-to-face conversation, phone calls, letters, email, text messages, or something else? Why might you want to connect to these people and use these forms of communication with each one?

27

Healing through Conversation

"One often calms one's grief by recounting it."
Pierre Corneille

Question to Consider: Why does "talking it out" help?

Talking about personal problems is necessary, especially in a time of major grief, but guys often have a problem with it. We men often think we need to be strong and do things our own way without consulting others. This impulse can be isolating, especially when your wife's death has already set you apart from other men who are married or single with busy lives. You are not like these other men: you are a widow-man, and you need someone to talk with about this new life.

What issues of being a widow-man would you like to talk over with a person who would understand? Just writing about it here may help now, and it may prepare you for that conversation later.

You are adjusting to perhaps the biggest change of your life. Piecing together the shattered fragments of your life goes on silently inside you, but conversation is indispensable to that reconstruction. As you talk and listen, you become more comfortable with your new widow-man self.

To what extent can you modify your masculine tendency to be a "strong, silent type" and begin to talk with trusted friends or professionals about what you are going through?

Private conversations have been an important part of my recovery, in addition to my meetings with the grief group at my church. I have talked with family members and friends, and for a while I met with a professional counselor. I have had long phone conversations and hundreds of email exchanges with patient family members and friends.

What kind of person (family, friend, or professional) would you talk with most easily? How would you arrange that conversation?

Books and essays on grief have been part of my "conversation" with the larger world. In them I find people who understand even though I can't talk with them directly. Likewise, conversations with myself through journaling have been essential to my healing.

What "go-to" sources of reading do you have to help you through your recovery? How does writing in this journal help you understand your thoughts better?

Some aspects of grief are intensely personal. Missing the intimacy with your wife, for example, is not something you can talk about comfortably with your kids. Issues of guilt are another one. You don't want to "tell all" and later regret the conversation. On the other hand, pastors and counselors can listen to just about anything, and they have training and experience that can help you.

What aspects of your grief are best shared with family members, and what aspects might best be reserved for other conversations?

If you have children, even adult children, be judicious when talking with them about your grief. They are grieving too, and their grief is different from yours, partly because they knew their mother all their lives. With my children, it is sometimes sufficient just to agree with them when they say, "I miss Mom." I say, "I do too," and we are bonded in our grief without opening painful wounds.

How have you talked with your children about your grief and theirs? What do you wish you could convey to them?

Some aspects of grief recovery may require more than self-help and family conversations. If you find yourself chronically unable to sleep, eat, work, or enjoy anything in life, you probably need to seek professional help. It is a correct and manly thing to do. You may be amazed at the value of just a couple of meetings with the right professionally trained person.

Where can you seek professional help now or in the near future, should your grieving become unhealthy?

28

Healing by Helping Others

"Do not let your left hand know what your right hand is doing."
Matthew 6:3

Question to Consider: How can I get outside myself and help others?

Some widow-men and widows I know have grown in ways they hadn't before their spouses died. They had full lives with their spouses; they were not being held back in their marriages, but their new life has offered new opportunities.

One widow-man is legendary for sending greeting cards and notes to people who are sick, in grief, or in anxiety over work issues or personal conflicts. The same man has gone on several church work camps where he took risks to be immensely helpful.

Who could you help or encourage in the next few weeks? What would it take: an email, a phone call, a personal visit, a gift in the mail, food delivery, or the offer of transportation?

A widow turned her attention to Africa soon after her husband's death and has helped hundreds of widows and children there. She has involved other Americans as short-term volunteers as well. Working for a few days or weeks where people are surrounded by abject poverty has changed her life as well as the lives of these volunteers. Another widow has written inspiring articles and a book for widows.

What service opportunities could you consider? What would it take for you to be able to go on a short-term mission trip or be part of work camp?

You might at first think it is selfish to help others in order to deal with your own grief. I can assure you, those who are receivers of your help will not think you are being selfish. Also, while helping others, you are likely to learn positive things about that self of yours. It's okay to reach out to others you can help, even if you know it is partly therapy for you.

What specific things could you do to encourage at least two other people? What small things could you do soon?

About a year before my wife died, as I was getting dressed for one of my final days in the office, I said, "What am I going to do with all these suits after I retire? I won't need to wear suits to work anymore."

Without a pause, she said, "You keep all those suits. You're going to need them for all the funerals you're going to be attending."

We both laughed, but she had in fact named one of my new "jobs." I'm not exactly a professional mourner, but I do attend a lot of funerals, the visitations that precede them, and the family dinners that follow. It has become one of my "ministries," a work God prompts me to do to serve him and others.

Now that you are a widow-man familiar with grief and loss, how has this time of grief prepared you to "mourn with those who mourn"?

About a month after my wife died, a former colleague of hers, a widow herself, sent me a book of daily meditations called *Healing after Loss* by Martha Whitmore Hickman. The book was immensely helpful to me, and I have made a practice of sending it to newly widowed men and women I know. Some of them now send the book on to others.

What could you give to a grieving friend that would show your sympathy and help him in his grief?

29

In Sickness and in Health

"I praise you, for I am fearfully and wonderfully made."
Psalm 139:14

Question to Consider: Who will care for me now?

The traditional wedding vow includes a pledge to care for each other "in sickness and in health." While your wife lived, you both fulfilled the "in sickness" part of this vow in your own ways and in your own circumstances. You enjoyed the "in health" portion much more, doing things together as a married couple. And you fulfilled that other portion of the wedding vow, "till death do us part," by remaining married until her death. Now that she's gone, you must care for yourself in sickness and in health.

How did you fulfill the "in sickness" portion of the wedding vow during your wife's lifetime? What plans and provisions can you put in place now for your care in case of illness?

Most people think of the "in sickness" part of this vow more than the "in health" portion. Your responsibility now is not only to doctor yourself back to health when something goes wrong, but also to care for yourself "in health." Even if you sometimes don't feel much like extending your life by good health habits, they can help you recover from your grief and have energy to explore new activities.

Self-care includes regular medical checkups, completing courses of medication when needed, disposal of out-of-date medications, use of a hat and sunscreen outdoors, and disposal of long-expired food. (My children will laugh at that last item. I am notorious for eating food that has been in the house too long.)

What actions do you need to commit to as part of your self-care plan?

Regular exercise is essential to your well-being and health at any age. It also shows others that you are caring for yourself. I'm not an athlete, but I have learned that I can do most things better if I have some exercise nearly every day. Walking is the most essential part of my exercise routine. Other widow-men I know jog for exercise or play golf, tennis, or racquetball.

What form of exercise did you enjoy in the past? What are you doing now? What have you considered adding?

If there is a fountain of youth, its name is "exercise." In the first year after my wife's death, I responded to a challenge from a friend and explored local gyms. I had never used a gym since high school physical education class, so this was a big step. I found a gym with a seniors discount and began to use resistance machines for upper body conditioning. Visits to the gym two or three times each week have built my morale and even some visible muscle.

What would attract you to a gym membership? What would deter you?

A widow friend told me I would either gain or lose a lot of weight after my wife died. I was thankful for her warning, but my weight has remained steady. Three years earlier I had joined Weight Watchers and lost some weight, which I have managed to keep off through a good enough diet and regular exercise. I still follow some of the basic Weight Watchers rules, and I weigh myself daily, just as we did at the weekly "weigh in" at Weight Watchers.

How do you "weigh in" right now? What have you done in the past to control your weight? What might you try in the next three months?

30

Your Wedding Ring

"With this ring, I thee wed."

Question to Consider: Shall I continue to wear my wedding ring?

My wife and I wanted only simple gold wedding bands. She had never wanted an ornate engagement ring, and we did not have much money to invest in rings anyway. We bought our wedding rings at an Indianapolis jewelry store shortly before we were married in June 1971. We paid $25 for both rings, and we always delighted in telling people how cheap they were: "Two for twenty-five dollars," we often explained. In August 1971, the price of gold was deregulated and the price of gold skyrocketed. If we had bought the rings and married three months later, the cost could have been hundreds of dollars.

We wore our rings continuously until June 1974, when we were in the San Fernando Valley doing some technical rock climbing. I was going to try a difficult move. To avoid snagging my ring on the rock, I told her I needed to take my ring off. My wife and I hesitated, took a deep breath, and had a little ceremony of mutually removing our rings at the same moment. We always remembered that moment and how much it had meant to have worn our rings nonstop for three years. Many more years followed, and we rarely removed our rings.

How did you and your wife decide upon the rings you bought?

A few minutes after my wife died, I slipped the wedding ring from her finger and placed it securely in my wallet. Within a couple of weeks, I bought a small safe in which to store things related to my wife's life and death, including her ring.

What to do about my wife's ring seemed clear to me, but I wasn't so sure what to do about mine. In the short run, it was easy to continue wearing it, so that's what I did. The ring didn't fill me with grief; on the contrary, it was a consoling presence, a reminder of the security I had felt in our marriage. It was also a signal to others that I was still bound to my wife even though she had died.

What did you do with your wife's ring and other jewelry? What thoughts come to you when you glance at your wedding ring?

I continued to wear my wedding ring as comfortably and unconsciously as I had when my wife was alive until the middle of my first year without her. In spite of my vow not to get involved with women that year, one day I found myself chatting, maybe even flirting, with a check-out woman in a store. I didn't know her at all. When I got home, I thought about what I had done. I had been wearing my wedding ring. What did she think? What did others around us think? Did it appear to her or others that I was a married man out flirting with another woman?

The next day, I made a point of taking off my wedding ring. I found that woman and explained that I was not married, that my wife had died, and that I had still been wearing my wedding ring. She accepted my explanation, but I'll never know if she believed it.

Why do you need to be aware of what your wedding ring says to the world? What explanation do you offer others about wearing or not wearing it?

I kept my wedding ring off for several months after that incident. Doing so avoided the unsavory implication of being a married man on the make whenever I talked with other women. I know several widows who still wear their wedding rings, partly to fend off unwelcome advances by men. I suspect there are widow-men who continue to wear their rings for the same reason: to avoid unwanted romantic contacts. There must be widow-men whose rings are an unwelcome reminder of their loss, and they may put their rings away for that reason.

What rules of "ring etiquette" do you think you will adopt in the coming months and years? How will you know when it's time to stop wearing your wedding ring?

31

Looking Back on Marriage

"Therefore a man shall leave his father and his mother and hold
fast to his wife, and they shall become one flesh."
Genesis 2:24

Question to Consider: What can I learn about marriage now?

My wife and I had a wonderful, strong marriage. We were married thirty-nine years before she died, and we raised three children who are responsible Christian adults with excellent marriages. I always felt that it was God's will for me to be married to my wife, and I'm sure she felt the same. Friends have sometimes commented on the quality of our marriage, and I am always thankful for what they saw in the two of us together.

After I became a widow-man, I found myself thinking a lot about marriage in general and my marriage in particular. I thought back over many scenes from my own marriage, and I looked at other people's marriages with a curiosity I never had before. I listened to things people said about their spouses, and I observed their behavior together. I had a lot to learn about marriage.

I continue to think about and observe marriages. I am impressed with the complexity of marriage. I can see that complexity better now that I am no longer involved in the sharing, the compromises, and the occasional conflicts and irritations in even the best marriages. My parents had a wonderful marriage of sixty-nine years, but even they had their moments of exasperation. I continue to try to understand that most important episode of my life.

What do you understand better now than ever before about your own marriage, other marriages you know, and marriage in general?

When I think about marriage in general, I sometimes envision the marriage partners as two ships traveling parallel to each other in the open sea. During courtship they move closer to each other, and in marriage they tie their ships together with strong ropes. The ships are bound closely together for the duration of the journey, but they are still separate ships with separate lives onboard. Occasionally the ships collide and sometimes they tend to pull apart, but the ropes still hold if all goes well. Sometimes the crew of one ship may try to board the other, invading its space, and new rules of engagement have to be developed for continued happiness on the journey.

What images of marriage come to your mind? Were you and your wife separate ships, or were you more like the crew of a single vessel, both "in the same boat"?

One of the most helpful books I read after my wife's death was *Healing after Loss*, by Martha Whitmore Hickman. It's a series of meditations for every day of the year. In the book, the author advises, "It is unwise, because it is untrue, to idealize the dead. . . . The myth of perfection is hard to maintain. We do not need it. We can give it over—to God, if you will. Lay it down. Leave it there." The author goes on to say that our wives were God's children, just as they were. They were loved and acceptable, and so are we.

Why is it important to be truthful with yourself about your wife and about your marriage—its good parts and its shortcomings? Why is it important to be judicious about how widely you share those thoughts?

A friend of mine once shocked me by saying that one trait of a perfect marriage is that you are sometimes angry at each other. I have often observed couples who appear to have "perfect" marriages, and I now "read between the lines" to realize that there surely must be occasional disagreements and irritations even within those wonderful marriages. It makes me wonder what others thought about my marriage.

Did your children and your friends think you had a perfect marriage? Whether they did or not, what were the strengths and stresses a close observer would have seen in your marriage?

I think the movie *About Schmidt* gives an especially meaningful view of widow-men. The main character, played by Jack Nicholson, loses his wife early in the movie. The rest of the movie shows him finding his place in his new, difficult life. At one point, thinking about his deceased wife, he asks himself, "What did she really think of me?"

How do you think your wife saw the marriage you shared? What did she value the most and the least?

32

Dreams

"An angel of the Lord appeared to him in a dream, saying, 'Joseph,
son of David, do not fear to take Mary as your wife.'"
Matthew 1:20

Question to Consider: What do dreams of her mean?

Dreams have fascinated mankind since long before Joseph's dreams, recorded in the Old Testament, saved Egypt from an agricultural disaster. Dreams continue to fascinate us, though there is no settled scientific or psychological agreement on exactly what they are.

When my wife was alive, we often told each other our dreams the next morning. My dreams were usually vivid but brief and absurd. My wife's dreams were amazingly detailed, complex, and long. They too seemed pointless, but it was fun to see where our minds had taken us while we slept.

What did you and your wife tell each other about your dreams? Was there any difference between her dreams and yours?

For many widow-men, dreams are especially interesting because we sometimes see our wives in them. Two elderly widow-men with whom I have corresponded about this book have told me that they often dream of their deceased wives. One of those men had been married sixty-seven years, and his marriage continues in his dreams. The other had been married for fifty-three years. Even though he remarried and his second wife also died, he says he invariably is with his first wife in his dreams.

Why do you suppose these men dream so much of their wives? How often do you dream about you and your wife together?

I do not believe my dreams hold any prophetic power. My dreams amaze me, but not for their insights into tomorrow's events or even into past events. The things that creep into my dreams usually seem random. They are sometimes very detailed and deal with things I have never seen, experienced, or thought about before. Other people say they receive guidance or insights from their dreams that are helpful in the present. One person I know prays before bed for dreams that will bring insights about her past and help her resolve lingering feelings of false guilt.

I seldom dreamed about my wife in the first year after her death. To my surprise, I dreamed about her more in the second year and even more in the third year. My dreams of her are usually very brief, and they mainly convey a feeling of her presence. Sometimes I see her doing things she never would have done in real life, like over-salting her food. Twice my dreams were quite complex and contained separate dreams within them.

How often do you dream about your wife? How soon after her death did you begin to dream about her?

Unlike most of my dreams, the ones about my wife do seem to convey a meaning or a message. These are not prophetic messages about the future, but they almost always convey meaning about the past. In my dreams I sometimes see my wife close up: I see her skin color and texture, her hair, her mouth. Sometimes I dream of her saying something, but usually I just feel her presence. In those moments, I feel restored to my marriage. For me these dreams are affirmations of my marriage, almost like Joseph's New Testament dream of an angel affirming that he should take Mary, the mother of Jesus, as his wife. In those dreams, I feel married and assured of her presence, and that assurance often remains when I awaken.

Are your dreams of your wife like a pleasant gift, or do they make you sad? Do any of those dreams seem prophetic, providing insight for something in your future?

You may be wondering if my dreams of my wife are romantic or intimate. I have had only one such dream, and it was more than three years after my wife died. When I mentioned to one of my daughters (a mother in her thirties) that I'd had a romantic dream about her mother, she covered her ears and shouted, "TMI! TMI!" (Too much information!) So I stopped at that point, and I'll stop here for your sake too.

If you can remember interesting dreams about your wife that you want to savor in the future, make a few notes here.

33

Your Wife's Legacy

"So Rachel died and was buried on the way to Ephratha (that is, Bethlehem). Over her tomb Jacob set up a pillar, and to this day that pillar marks Rachel's tomb."
Genesis 35:19-20 (NIV)

Question to Consider: What is important for people to know about my wife and her life?

A *legacy* is something received from or transmitted by someone from the past or from someone who has died. Physical objects or financial assets can be part of a legacy, but here I'm more interested in our wives' spiritual, intellectual, and moral legacies. I'm interested in identifying those stories for which our wives will be known.

You are now the custodian of your wife's legacy. You know more about her than anyone, and the knowledge of who she was and what she did in her life is part of her legacy. There probably are things about her that you haven't thought about for some time, and some are important for her children and grandchildren to know.

What stories about your wife's life come to mind immediately? What will your children and grandchildren need to know about her that you alone can tell?

My wife was clear-eyed about people's memories of the departed. She often said, "The wake closes quickly after you are gone," referring to people leaving their jobs as well as people leaving this earth. She would not be surprised to find people's memories of her fading quickly, yet I want her to be remembered, at least for a while longer, at least by our children and grandchildren.

About two months before my wife died, she said her only real regret about dying "so soon" was that she wouldn't know her grandchildren and they wouldn't know her. She accepted the reality of her approaching death calmly, but she didn't necessarily want to vanish from the minds of those she loved and those she would never meet because they were yet to be born.

On my wife's second to last day of conscious life, our family had gathered around her at the hospital. My son told her that he and his wife were expecting their first child, her fifth grandchild. Joy spread across her face, anticipating that future life she wouldn't live to see.

On her last day of conscious life, our children brought the four grandchildren to the hospital for her to see once more. She touched each one, and if they were willing, she hugged them. It was like Jacob in the Genesis account, blessing his children before his death.

What are your most important memories of your wife's last conversations with you and your family? If you were unable to be there at the moment she died, what do you wish your parting conversation would have been?

When I was a boy under ten years old, I was fascinated by the old photographs of my parents' grandparents. Some were born before the Civil War, and many had been pioneers. Those photos and the stories passed on to me by my parents are part of my heritage. I want my grandchildren to know even more about my wife and me.

What parts of your wife's legacy do you think she especially would want to be shared? Why does sharing her legacy matter to you?

Three months before my wife died, she requested a beautiful journaling book, *Conversations with My Mother*, published by Lark Books. The book is a guided tour through one's life and also the lives of the writer's parents and grandparents. My wife used that book as her own journaling guide and made many entries before she died. That journal was her way of passing along her legacy to her children and grandchildren. After she died, I placed her journaling book in my fireproof safe. Four months after her death, I took it to a print shop and had copies made for my three kids, my wife's two sisters, and the nieces and nephews on her side of the family.

What did your wife do to share her legacy with her family? What ideas do you have to add to what she did?

In the companion book, *Conversations with My Father,* I made many entries on evenings while my wife was writing in her book. We would often check with each other on details or enjoy reminding each other of memories that the journaling books had awakened. If you are interested in this approach, you could use that same journaling book to convey your life story to your children and grandchildren. You could also buy *Conversations with My Mother* and complete as much of it as possible in honor of your wife.

How do you feel about using these books as a legacy gift for your children and grandchildren?

34

Stages of Life

"For everything there is a season, and a time
for every matter under heaven."
Ecclesiastes 3:1

Question to Consider: In what stage of life am I now living?

Life does have its seasons. Your life can be divided into at least three broad time periods: before marriage, during marriage, and after marriage—single, married, and widowed. You are now in a period of life that you didn't expect, and it's a stage that your wife didn't experience: widowhood.

What would widowhood have been like for your wife if you had died first? How would she spend a day like today?

In the last year of her life, my wife reflected on our years in Wisconsin, where all of our children were born and where I made a major career change. We had been married only three years when we moved there. She was twenty-eight when we arrived and forty-six when we left; I was thirty-four when we arrived and fifty-two when we left. Near the end of her life, she said, "Those years were the summertime of our lives."

What was the summertime of your life with your wife? What stands out in your mind?

When I was a young boy with almost no knowledge of sex or married life, I already looked forward to being a married man. That hope continued through my teenage years and early adulthood. Perhaps I idealized marriage, but I later formed a more mature idea of what it can be.

How did your childhood and teenage years prepare you to be a married man? What events shaped your attitude toward marriage when you were in your teens and twenties?

Over the forty-five years I knew my wife, I learned a lot about her life in the years before we met. I learned of the devout Christian girl she had been and of the diligent student she was all her life. As I came to know her, I could see how her spiritual nature and intellectual discipline had held me on course in a way that would have been unlikely without her. Perhaps I brought some interesting unpredictability to her life! The earlier stages of our lives prepared us for our marriage and made it strong.

What experiences in your earlier lives prepared you and your wife for the marriage you shared? How did meeting her and dating change your life and your ideas about marriage?

Even before my wife's first cancer diagnosis, we had talked fleetingly about one of us surviving the other. We assumed, of course, that I would die first because I was six years older, and men tend to die younger than women. It seemed likely that she would be a widow, perhaps for many years. We had vague ideas about what life would be like for the survivor in each case. We thought about care for our children and whether the survivor would remarry.

What did you and your wife think about life for either of you in widow-hood? In what ways is your widowhood like or different from the expectations you formed earlier?

This stage of life won't go on forever. Your grief will change, and your marital status might change. Just as marriages end in death or divorce, widowhood can end in death or remarriage. Within the months and years of your widow-man time, much can happen.

What do you expect from your life in the next five years? What are the main things you expect about your health, employment, finances, children and other family relationships, women, remarriage, housing, travel, fun, sadness, and illness?

PART THREE

35

Money Matters

"Wisdom is a shelter as money is a shelter, but the advantage of
knowledge is this: Wisdom preserves those who have it."
Ecclesiastes 7:12 (NIV)

Question to Consider: How will I manage my money now?

The Teacher in Ecclesiastes advises us that "money is a shelter," but he indirectly cautions that money in itself doesn't preserve us as wisdom does. Money is only a tool, but it's a uniquely important tool.

I have held this chapter until late in the book on the assumption that some of your financial adjustments are longer-term concerns than most of the topics covered earlier. I am not a financial advisor, though I employ one to help with my financial decisions. I recommend that you find someone with whom you can talk in confidence about your finances, even if you have some expertise in this area. For objectivity if nothing else, a professional advisor, a family member, a friend, or perhaps even someone on your church staff can help. Be sure this person is able to talk with you analytically without a personal stake in your decisions.

How often do you review your finances on your own? How often do you consult someone who knows more than you?

Your tolerance for risk probably has changed since your wife's death. You may need or want to reduce the degree of risk in your financial holdings. If you haven't evaluated your finances recently, you may want to make changes in your assets, insurance, and debt management. Advancing age alone leads to changes in the optimal handling of finances.

What financial matters are already on your mind? In what ways are they new now because of your age, your employment, or the fact that you are a widow-man?

One of the largest financial decisions for widow-men and widows is housing. If you and your wife were living in your own house, you may soon wonder if there is another place you should consider. Emotional issues as well as financial questions are important here. Is your present home convenient and a comfort to you? Is it a place where your children grew up and perhaps come to visit with their families several times a year? On the other hand, does your home stir negative emotions or is it becoming unwieldy to manage?

What are your thoughts for and against moving to another home or another housing arrangement?

For at least the first year after your wife's death, it's probably wise not to sell your house and move unless economic pressure forces it on you. After that first year, you will be able to look at the question with more objectivity. I still live in the house we bought twenty years ago, and I love it here. My children love to come here, and the grandchildren enjoy the spaces for play. Yet a time is approaching when I won't have the stamina or even the desire to maintain this house. I might not even be safe here or able to climb the stairs.

If you haven't downsized already, how will you know when it's time?

A popular way to downsize is to move to a senior living community. I know many people both older and younger than I who have made this move happily, and I can see advantages in the simplification senior living can bring. When my health begins to fail, as it will, I'll want to have people nearby and possibly even medical support in the place where I'll live. I hope I will have the presence of mind to make the decision to move when I need to.

What appeals to you about a senior living place now? What is unappealing?

You probably already have begun to review your insurance needs. Your home and auto insurance may not need special attention, but medical insurance, Medicare supplements, life insurance, and long-term care insurance will need to be updated soon. This can lead you into a number of complex questions for which a professional advisor can be a great help. See the Internet to begin schooling yourself on the complex subject of insurance.

Where can you get the advice you need to evaluate your insurance coverage?

36

Retirement

"When you are retired, you never get a day off."
Nyle Kardatzke

Question to Consider: How will I spend my time in retirement?

Most of what I have written in this journaling book has been pitched to older men (over sixty) for the obvious reason that most widow-men are in that age range. If you haven't retired already, it's something you probably have thought about. If you are retired, your retirement years present new questions after your wife's death.

Retirement involves our emotional and spiritual needs as well as financial questions. I'm retired, but I am not a big fan of retirement as the be-all, end-all of life for everyone. But I don't deny that retirement can be a blessed "gift of time," even after the loss of your wife. The greatest benefit I have found in retirement is having fewer fixed duties on my calendar and more flexibility in most of my days. Emotional downsides of retirement include loneliness away from colleagues and anxiety over decreased income. A spiritual aspect of retirement is that you must find something else to define your life and shape your daily activities. While you are employed, your job provides a lot of your identity. Without your job, identity questions loom large.

If you are employed, why might you continue working, at least for a while? What forces or feelings attract you to retirement, and which might make you wait? What does your decision have to do with the loss of your wife? If you are retired, what emotional and spiritual aspects of retirement do you find challenging now that your wife has died?

I retired at age seventy, exactly one year and ten days before my wife died. I am thankful we had that year, and I'm thankful I am able now to devote time to my children, grandchildren, other family members, friends, church, and other personal interests. Although I loved my work, my retirement time is another kind of "job" in which I monitor my time and use it in the most valuable ways I can manage. I have told a few friends that being retired, for me, is another kind of management job.

If you are retired, how did you choose the time to quit? What have been the greatest advantages in being retired? What regrets do you have about when you retired? If you are not retired, what vision of retirement do you have that will give you a new identity and sense of worth?

There are times when I think wistfully of the joys of having a job, surrounded by fellow workers and energized by goals, deadlines, and the financial rewards of working. If I had a job, it might take my mind off my wife's death. I have thought about "un-retiring" and taking a job for all the reasons I just named, but so far I'm still retired.

If you are retired, what might cause you to "un-retire" and take a new job? What might hold you back from that decision? How would a job be helpful to you in your grief? If you are not retired, what do you need to think about to ensure your retirement will be under favorable circumstances to you?

People are living much longer than they were fifty years ago. They also tend to be in better health than their grandparents were at their age. Longer life implies a need for more money during retirement; better health implies an opportunity to work and earn longer.

How has your health and longevity shaped your thoughts of retirement? What ideas about retirement did you and your wife share?

I'm over seventy. I'm in good health, but basic upkeep of my body takes more time than when I was a lot younger. Since health problems are important factors for retirement, they compel some men to keep their jobs for the sake of health insurance coverage.

What health considerations affect your thoughts about retirement?

Retirees nearly always say they are busy, and most say they don't know how they ever had time to hold a job. You probably have seen your parents or others retire and become busier than ever. I sometimes joke that I must not have been doing anything productive when I was "working" since I'm so busy now. I hope I'm joking about that.

Why do you suppose retirees say they are so busy? If you are not yet retired, what do you think will keep you busy in retirement? If you are retired, how do you manage your time?

37

Your Adult Children

"And he will turn the hearts of fathers to their chil-
dren and the hearts of children to their fathers."
Malachi 4:6

Question to Consider: What do my adult children and I provide each other?

Your adult children have suffered a great loss, too. You probably have done what you could to comfort them and give them wisdom about life without their mother. The fact remains, however, that they are without their mother and the things she used to do with them and for them. It's important for you to continue to think about them and their needs, just as you did when they were younger.

They may turn to you for more parental attention than if your wife were here, or they may pull away from you to deal with their grief, recovery, and adulthood in their own ways.

In what ways have your relationships with each of your children changed since your wife's death? What are you doing differently now in your relationships with them?

My wife had close relationships with our three children and their spouses. She would talk with them at great length about their wedding plans, apartment decorations, careers, and babies. At times I felt a little jealous about her attention to them, but I was also happy to see the joy she and the children had in each other.

She was an expert in child development and in parenting, and when our children became parents, she shared that expertise with our daughters and our daughter-in-law. Overhearing her side of the phone conversations, I was amazed at her wisdom and knowledge. Since she died, we have all wished we could ask her advice about the grandchildren. I'm a poor substitute for her in that area, but I'm doing my best to learn more as I go along.

How would you describe your wife's relationship with your children? What expertise of hers was most valuable to your children?

I think that grandmothers are usually more nurturing than grandfathers, and mothers typically are more closely involved in the lives of their children than are the fathers. But fathers and grandfathers play their own special roles. Sometimes just "being there" either in person or on the phone or computer is what is needed. Above all, "being there" means paying attention and listening, even to some things you don't understand. I have learned that my two-year-old grandchildren delight in my attention, even if they sometimes don't seem to notice me. The older grandchildren need more concrete evidence that I'm paying attention. You're not finished yet!

What are some of the things your children remember most about your parenting of them? What is most important about your father figure and grandfather figure roles now?

At Christmastime three years after my wife died, one of my daughters began quizzing me on my wishes for my care when my health begins to fail. At the time my health was excellent, but it would have been absurd to pretend that my mental and physical health will continue in the same condition for another thirty years.

Since that time I have talked with my children about some of my future hopes for health, independence, and adequate care if I decline gradually rather than die suddenly. It was a major step toward their taking over a parental concern for me. We have not resolved many issues, but it was an important conversation. I need to continue that conversation with my children as my age increases and my health changes.

What do you need to tell your children about your hopes and plans for a time when you are not as strong and alert as you are now? When might be a good time to have that conversation?

38

Grandparenting Alone

"Grandchildren are the crown of the aged, and the glory
of children is their fathers."
Proverbs 17:6

Question to Consider: How can I grandparent so my grandchildren have the attention they need from me?

It's true that once we become parents, we are parents as long as we live. Our parenting role calls for special awareness now that we are alone. Being the sole grandparent on your side of your grandchildren's lives presents some delightful opportunities and a few challenges. You may need to learn some tricks of grandparenting that your wife would have handled alone or with your help.

If your first grandchild was born after your wife's death, you probably grieved your wife's loss in a new way: she would not be grandparenting with you, and she wouldn't even know this new generation of family.

I personally think God intended grandfathers to die before grandmothers because grandmothers are so much more nurturing than grandfathers. When I remember the attention my wife gave our grandchildren, it's easy to see they would have better attention now if I had died first. Grandfathers tend to be rather matter-of-fact and show affection at the appointed times: birthdays, Christmas, and the like. But grandmothers seem always to be on the job, and they generally look more deeply and warmly into the grandchildren's lives than grandfathers. I consider myself a pretty good grandfather, but I'm only rating myself in the bush league.

What do you think is most important about your role as a grandfather? How has your role changed since your wife died?

When I'm around my grandchildren and their parents, I'm often thankful that I'm not the person in charge. The grandchildren are even more energetic than I remember my children being, and they need even more continuous attention than I remembered being true for my children. I sometimes have to remind myself that I'm not the parent of my grandchildren, only the grandfather, and I need to hold my tongue if I think I would do something different in managing the children.

How do you remain patient when your children don't manage your grandchildren the way you think they should? What do you especially admire about your children's parenting of their children?

I visit my adult children's homes a few times each year for varying lengths of time, depending partly on how far away they live: the greater the distance, the longer the visit. When I'm in their homes, I try to find useful things to do so I'm not just another person they have to care for. I have found that setting and clearing the table, washing dishes, folding laundry, doing carpool runs, grocery shopping, making my bed, picking up after myself, and telling bedtime stories are among the most useful things I can do.

What would make you an especially welcome houseguest in your adult children's homes?

I sometimes tell my own stories to the grandchildren at bedtime, and I have written some of those stories. In telling and reading these stories, I occasionally mention my wife as "Grandma Darlene" to keep her present and to put her name into their vocabularies. It means something to me, and it may mean something to them in future years. I mention her in a cheerful or factual way, not with any sadness.

What stories of yours would you like to tell your grandchildren? How can you include your wife's name in the stories so that the story-telling becomes a gift in memory of her?

I fall short in thinking of gifts for my grandchildren; my wife would have done so much better. I have been helped greatly by my children and in-law children in thinking of gifts for the grandkids. I usually remember the major occasions such as Christmas, but birthdays can sneak past me. Even with their suggestions, I'm not good at determining the best size or price for gifts. Clothing can be a challenge, and toy buying is difficult when they already seem to have all the toys they could possibly want.

How can a widow-man gain the skills needed give good gifts to his grandchildren?

If you love children and wish you had more grandchildren or more time with grandchildren, you could become a surrogate grandfather to other children in your family network or in your neighborhood. My children still love "Grandpa Bud" and "Grandma Edna," neighbors in Wisconsin when my children were young. Bud and Edna acted as grandparents to my children when their natural grandparents lived hundreds of miles away. A birthday card or a small gift from a "grandpa" like you can dazzle a child or even an adult. You can enjoy some of the joys of parenthood and grandparenting in creative ways without having full responsibility!

What child could you surprise this year with a card or a gift?

39

Love and Companionship

"God is love."
1 John 4:16
"All things were made through him."
John 1:3
"In Him all things hold together."
Colossians 1:17
"Two are better than one."
Ecclesiastes 4:9

Question to Consider: How shall I act on my need for love and companionship?

Some of the same urges that led us to marry may lead us to seek love and companionship again. We were created to be loving beings, and we are social beings, even if we sometimes want to be alone. The word *love* is so overworked that it can become trite, even boring. But the concept of love attempts to grasp perhaps the greatest reality about life.

It is important to distinguish between actual love and the state of being "in love." Thanks to Hollywood, we also need to be clear that love is not the same thing as sex or falling in love, though they are intertwined. While we widow-men may feel sexual desire, and we might

158

even "fall in love" again, I believe the love we seek is something deeper and more profound.

How would you describe the relationship of love to sexual desire, being "in love," and "falling in love"?

Love, it seems to me, is a magnetic or gravitational force that arose from God at the creation. The Bible says, "God is love," and concerning Jesus, "All things were made through him . . . and in him all things hold together." So I think love permeates the cosmos, holding galaxies and solar systems together, wrapping our planet in life-giving oxygen and binding men, women, and children together in families and societies. We shouldn't be surprised that we continue to feel a pull toward God and toward other people, and especially toward some with whom we could share years of life.

What do you think love is? How is love in general different from marital love?

Companionship is talked of less than love, yet it's closely related. I used to hear men talk of their wives as their "best friends." That idea was foreign to me. Marriage for me was more binding and more all-encompassing than any friendship I could imagine, and it came with more accountability. Friendships, in contrast, create strong and delightful bonds, but they are more easily started and stopped than marriages. And not all friendships are intended to last a lifetime.

After my wife died, I began to think of our love and companionship and the natural flow of activity between us. It was only then I realized my wife had in fact been my best friend.

What memories cause you to think of your wife as your best friend? What kind of friendship do you now seek in others, perhaps especially in women?

More than three years after my wife died, I awoke one morning with a feeling of loneliness. I thought, *I need a companion, but I don't know how to have a constant companion now.* Then I thought, *The Lord is my companion.* I went on to another thought: "The Lord is my shepherd" (Psalm 23:1). I knew I hadn't made up that last thought, and so I was reminded that I had companionship beyond what I might find with another human being, even beyond what I had known in marriage.

How do you feel about God's companionship now compared to how you thought about it before your wife died? What do you now seek in human companionship?

40

Dating

"Seek, and you will find."
Luke 11:9

Question to Consider: Will I venture into the world of women again by dating?

Dating may not be the right word for what a widow-man might do in search of female companionship. Among younger people, dating seems to go on more rapidly and more casually than when I was dating women in my young adulthood. Fewer rules seem to apply today, and there are more venues for meeting women than ever.

If you are over forty and thinking about dating, you might want to know that some people will find it strange to think of you as having a "girlfriend." If you are over seventy, it may seem stranger still, even comical, to others and to yourself. And the truth is, there are differences for between male-female companionship now and the dating we knew as young men. But having a "girlfriend" and dating in some form will be needed if you feel a pull toward a special friendship with one woman.

What are your thoughts about dating again, after all these years? If you've tried it, how did it feel compared to when you were seventeen or twenty?

I have had little experience with dating since my widowhood began. Most of my social contacts with women in my age range have been with widows and divorced women who are not interested in dating. Few women my age have remained unmarried all their lives. Divorced women seem so much like widows that I think of them as "virtual widows."

What are your experiences socializing with women your age now? When, if ever, will you be ready to consider dating rather than just socializing?

Simply meeting women is the first challenge of dating. Meeting at church, on the job, or through friends may still be the best ways to connect with women your age, and there are far more ways to follow up than in the "old days": email, text messages, Facebook, and the ever-present cell phone with caller ID and voicemail are a few. Old-fashioned greeting cards or letters in the mail are options, and they can seem more personal than the modern electronic methods.

"Computer dating" existed back in the 1960s, but online dating is much more sophisticated now. There are so many online dating sites now that you need to investigate carefully if you want to try this. I know several men who have found wives online with whom they are happy today, so it can work successfully. Meeting women online does not necessarily mean you plan to marry them; it can be just for dinner or for a night at the movies.

How would you want to meet a woman to date? Where would you go on a date?

Dating has become more casual than when I was a young man, and the expectations have changed. On the one hand, it seems easier now to have a truly casual date for dinner and a movie with no expectation of an ongoing relationship. Many women wouldn't want any other kind of date. At the other extreme, many people assume that a date will lead rapidly to sexual activity. Women are often wary of men seeking dates because of this heightened expectation. You also need to realize that some women you meet may have more aggressive plans than yours.

How will you communicate your trustworthiness to a woman you want to see socially? How will you avoid being led into an awkward situation by a woman?

41

A Celibate Life

"To the unmarried and the widows I say that it is
good for them to remain single as I am."
1 Corinthians 7:8

Question to Consider: Is my new, single life best for me for the rest of my life?

Very soon after my wife died, my mind whirled back to the day I met her many years earlier. I suddenly felt I was starting life over when I was twenty-five. My first impulse was to think I would soon go through some of the same stages: singleness; seeking, finding, loving, and marrying again; and building a life as a couple. It was a dizzying thought, and I set it aside.

I remembered my wife's advice not to get involved with women until at least a year after she died. I attempted to honor her advice. As time passed, I felt drawn more than once to women I knew, and I wondered if marriage might be in my future at some point. Then I drew back. I'm not sure now what my marital future may be.

If you have felt attracted to other women, how have you handled it thus far? How have your friendships with women affected your feelings about your single life?

Some Bible scholars think the apostle Paul may have been a widowman. He had to have been married at some point, since that was a requirement to be a member of the Sanhedrin, as he was. Some have speculated that his wife either died or divorced Paul when he became a Christian. He may have recommended singleness partly because of conflict in his marriage over his Christianity, as well as a way to focus on one's mission in life. Jesus did not marry, and he said "At the resurrection, people will neither marry nor be given in marriage; they will be like the angels in heaven" (Matthew 22:30 NIV). We widow-men have not entered heaven, but we have entered a life beyond the one we once knew. For some of us, this new life will best be lived in singleness.

What are your thoughts about embracing your single life? To what extent does it seem lonely and unstable? What advantages do you see for you in remaining single?

Being single does not always mean being celibate. You may already have heard seniors say, "The rules don't apply after age seventy!" You also may have heard about "arrangements" some seniors make to live together outside of marriage to preserve their retirement benefits, including healthcare, as well as securing their children's inheritances. But Christian morality as well as common sense recommends a choice: celibacy or marriage.

Aside from the practicality of managing your home and your social life alone, what challenges do you see in the single, celibate life?

Many of my diversions are homebound: reading, writing, Netflix movies, television, gardening, cooking, and correspondence. Other things I enjoy more with another person: travel, camping, long hikes, the symphony, art museums, and in-depth conversation. I haven't found a friend for most of my travel, and certainly not for camping and hiking.

If you remain single and celibate, what kind of social life do you hope for? Who are the friends, male and female, who make up the best parts of your social life now? If the social life you have is not yet enough to sustain you as a single, celibate man, how do you hope your life will change?

42

Remarriage

"He who finds a wife finds a good thing."
Proverbs 18:22

Question to Consider: Should I marry again?

Research shows that widow-men remarry more often and more quickly than widows. Some of the widow-men who previewed this book have remarried, and they all report happiness and peace in their new marriages. It's safe to say that the majority of widow-men consider remarriage soon after they lose their "better half."

I was surprised at how soon after my wife's death the question of remarriage arose. One or two people asked if I thought I would remarry, and I thought about it surprisingly soon myself. I could see that it was a possibility, that's all. I didn't feel guilty about having that thought because, after all, my wife was gone and I was no longer married. Also, my wife had made it clear that she assumed that I would marry after her death. She didn't urge it upon me; she simply stated it as a prediction.

An elderly widow once told me that at the burial of their wives, men are looking across the grave for their next wife. I prefer to think she didn't mean it literally, but when I see a widow-man remarry within a year or two after losing his wife, I wonder.

When, if ever, have you thought of marrying again? In what ways and why does that idea appeal to you or not?

If you are a younger widow-man, remarriage is a livelier question than for a much older man. You may want to start another family, or you may want to share the joy and work of parenting the children of the woman you marry. Or maybe you want the stability of being married again and having a sexual partner.

At any age you might welcome the idea of help with cooking and cleaning, but you may have heard that women are wary of men who mainly want a housekeeper. Older women are wary of men who want "a nurse and a purse." I have that on good authority.

For older widow-men, the desire for companionship can be strong, and some men may be desperate to escape the loneliness they feel. Strong emotions can lead to impulsive actions, and desperation is an emotion to be wary of in any situation. Friends who have remarried can tell you a new marriage is very different from the previous one, no matter how old or how young you are now.

What are some ways in which another marriage would be different from your first one?

When I think of remarriage for myself, I can see many practical differences between marrying after seventy and marrying for the first time in my twenties. And I can see differences in emotional issues. If you are like me, you probably have more property than when you first married, including a house. You may have financial assets, children, and grandchildren. If you think of marrying a woman in your age range, she quite likely will have a similar array of complications. The property, children, grandchildren, and extended families you would bring into a late-in-life marriage are blessings, but they also represent important complications.

If you remarry, another issue to resolve is with whom you will spend your holidays: her children and other family or yours?

What complications can you imagine in a remarriage for you?

The issues of a potential remarriage can surface sooner than you think. If you begin dating again, think especially of the possible reactions of your children and the children of the woman you are dating. Would they be suspicious of the motives of the two older, dating adults? When I was dating a woman after my wife's death, one of my daughters asked if the woman was going to "suck up all of your money" or if "you are going to suck up all of her money." This was her very direct way of voicing the concerns of adult children when one of their parents remarries late in life.

A recently remarried widow-man told me a pre-nuptial agreement is crucial in a remarriage, especially where adult children are involved. The same remarried widow-man has had to deal with the finances of his elderly, remarried father. He emphasized that a prenuptial agreement should take into account every imaginable event that could crop up in a new marriage, especially the costs of health care. All the questions you may have now about your own health care should be examined with respect to your future new wife, he said.

What practical issues can you foresee if you decide to remarry? What are the related diplomatic issues in your relationships with your children and other relatives?

I have read that when a widow or a widow-man remarries, she or he will always, in some ways, remain married to the first spouse. I know a widow-man who dated a widow after both their spouses died. They agreed early on in their dating that they would not pretend that her husband and his wife had never existed. That left them free to talk about them, and that made their previous spouses welcome and comfortable presences in the couple's dating. It was important for them to learn each other's histories, and those histories were filled with stories about their first marriages.

If you were to remarry, in what ways would your first wife remain with you? Would her "presence" help or hinder your new marriage? If you were to marry a widow, what would you want to know about her first husband and her marriage to him?

In the second year after my wife's death, a man who had remarried after a painful divorce gave a talk about his experience. One of his main points was that, especially when you marry later in life after a divorce, you marry not only your bride but also her entire family, and she is marrying your family. It's not a simple matter. The same is true for remarriage after the death of a spouse.

What would you hope to gain from another marriage? What would you offer your new wife? What challenges would you expect to face? How do you think your children and her children might view your late-in-life marriage?

43

Heaven

"Store up for yourselves treasures in heaven."
Matthew 6:20

Question to Consider: What is heaven like?

Thoughts of heaven are comforting to those who have lost a loved one in death. The promise of a life after this one softens the hurtful loss of the loved one's active presence here. Heaven is where my wife is cared for now, where her life is being fulfilled beyond anything imaginable here on the earth.

Widows I know and some widow-men like me need a personal picture of heaven, even if we don't know a lot of the details. Many people envision their departed loved ones in a permanent new life of health and youth. Within a Christian context, I think we can at least accept the assurance that heaven exists, is wonderful, and is the reward that God provides for his children. We can assume our spouses are there, and we might also then want to go on to imagine a picture of that new world and our loved one there.

How do you envision heaven and your wife there?

Will we have distinct personalities in heaven, or will we all be alike in some amorphous mass of happy spirits? Some believe that heaven will be so spiritual and so focused on God alone that we will no longer be identifiable beings. But the Bible places so much emphasis on individual human salvation, morality, and personality that I don't believe these aspects of humanity will be obliterated in heaven. True, our human nature and our personalities will be purified for life in heaven, but I think we will emerge there with a past as well as a present and a future.

In one of my last conversations with my wife, I said, "Even within the scale of human history, let alone the scale of all eternity, it will be only a short time before I join you in heaven." She quickly replied, "I'll be looking for you there." Clearly we both believed not only in the reality of heaven but also in our distinct personalities there.

How would you describe what you assume about the nature of human spirits in heaven?

In Scripture, Jesus says that in the resurrection, there will be neither marrying nor being given in marriage. I think this statement means marriage is an institution needed only here on earth, and new marriages will not be formed in heaven. I don't think it means our marriages here on earth will have no further meaning in heaven, or that we won't be able to find our spouses there. (Remember, these thoughts are from me, a widow-man, not Scripture.)

What do you think about the possibility of seeing your wife and greeting her in heaven? What about the experience of something like human emotions there?

A young girl in my church wrote a praise comment about God: "God is not bored." I had never before considered whether God could be bored, but I'm sure the answer must be no. But what about us? Could we get bored by eternity in heaven, even if we are with our wives? I think not. I think God's infinite beauty, truth, majesty, love, and creativity will keep us going forever. I think in heaven God will take away the earthly capacity for boredom. Heaven will be far more exciting than the common, though non-scriptural, view of people in white robes, floating on ethereal wings, and playing harps. And I think we will enjoy being with our wives as well as with God forever.

What do you like to think you might be able to do in heaven, and what do you think about the possibility of boredom there?

My wife believed that people in heaven might be able to see what is happening on the earth, at least part of it. She believed there might be a sort of polarized lens that would allow people in heaven to see life on the earth; but evil, violence, and sorrow would be filtered out. She thought people in heaven would be able to see joy and moments of goodness that foreshadow the joy and beauty of heaven to come.

What do you think about your wife being able to see you from heaven right now?

44

Your Life and Legacy

It is appointed for man to die once, and after that comes judgment."
Hebrews 9:27

Question to Consider: What will be my legacy?

I am almost reluctant to use the word *death,* even in in this chapter. In our culture these days, we talk of someone "passing" (a recent phenomenon) or "passing away" (a more traditional euphemism for death). Some refer to death as a "promotion to heaven" or "going to be with the Lord." Humorous to me, some people make a practice of saying, "If anything ever happens to me, . . ." as though nothing has ever happened to them before (and, if anything does happen, it will cause death).

Early in my widowhood, I decided to avoid euphemisms for death. Death deserves the dignity and majesty of its real name. My wife did not simply "pass." She had passed hundreds of exams in school, college, medical school, and beyond. She didn't just pass another test when she died. She didn't pass a test at all. She made the natural change from this life to the next, the greatest change we experience after emergence from the womb.

What words do you use to talk of your wife's death? How do you feel about using the "d word" related to her? How do you feel about saying "death" or "die" in reference to yourself?

I know I need to be aware that these remaining years may define me in the minds of my children and grandchildren more than my earlier years. Their memories of me will be the most important legacy I leave to my descendants.

How would you like to be remembered after you die? What can you do to shape those memories? How might this journaling book and other diaries and journals become part of the legacy you leave for your family?

My wife and I made notes about plans for our funerals and other death details three months before she died. In her last conscious day at the hospital, we reviewed those notes and formulated a nearly complete order of service for her memorial service. Even so, many decisions still had to be made after her death, and it became obvious to me how important it is to face end-of-life issues early on.

What can you do now to make your death easier for your family to handle?

Helping your family at the time of your death goes beyond an updated will and instructions about your funeral and burial or cremation. Emotional issues are important. You can ease their pain then by expressing your love for them now. You can work to resolve simmering conflicts when that's possible. Above all, you can tell your family members you love them and show it in all the ways you can.

Beyond the obvious, you can choose to live your life as fully as possible so they remember you as a lively, interesting person. You can tell them stories about your life. You can even write some of your stories to be handed down to future generations or have someone make a video of you telling or reading stories about yourself. Details about how you lived can become more interesting in future years. You may even want to write about your health issues, since those might figure into the health experiences of your children and grandchildren in the future.

What are the personal, emotional memories you want your family to have about you? What health matters do you need to be sure they know?

My aunt Marian was a widow for over ten years. Her husband, my uncle Paul, had achieved high military rank, and they lived in a suburb of Washington, D.C. Aunt Marian was athletic and self-determined, even in her late eighties. One night she had severe chest pains, so she did the obvious thing when going out for the evening in Washington: she called a cab and got nicely dressed. Her chest pains increased, and she barely made it to the cab before she collapsed. The shaken cab driver did what she should have done: he called 911. An ambulance arrived quickly, the medics checked Aunt Marian, and they determined she had died in the back seat of that cab.

What a way to go! She went in style, living out her life till the very last moments. She was full of life, faith, and confidence right down to that last walk to the taxi. Few of us will come to the end of our lives as dramatically as did Aunt Marian.

What can you do now to prepare, not only for your death, but also for the possibility of protracted illness and loss of functions before death comes?

45

The World after You and Me

*"For now we see through a glass, darkly; but then face to face: now I
know in part; but then shall I know even as also I am known."*
1 Corinthians 13:12 (KJV)

Question to Consider: What will the world be like after I'm gone?

A History Channel program shows details of the likely events on earth
if humans were to suddenly disappear. The program starts with the lives
of the surviving animals and plants. It moves on to the breakdown of
power plants and water supplies and the deterioration of homes and busi-
nesses. Animals initially invade abandoned homes for food and shelter,
but they soon go feral, becoming wild animals in their new ecology. The
program extends our imagination a few hundred years into the future
when very few traces of human activity would remain.

*Imagine what your residence and property could look like in fifty
years. Does your imagination give you any thoughts about what you
want to do with your home and belongings right now?*

184 | The World after You and Me

I somehow feel a kind of peace when I think of the world after my death. I'm comforted to imagine the world going on without me, utterly out of my control and beyond any responsibility of mine. Sometimes I have foreboding about the world my children and grandchildren will inherit, but I can't control the shape of that world, and I have only limited influence over how my children and grandchildren will prepare to live in it. All of the future is in God's hands, and that seems especially clear to me when I try to peer fifty or a hundred years ahead.

How do you picture the world after your death? How do you imagine, in the best possible scenarios, what each of your children and grandchildren will be like?

A famous book of meditations begins with the line, "It's not about you." That was the most powerful line in the entire book, I thought. This whole experience of life isn't about you or me but about a much larger body of life. Our lives are important to us and to God, but the world does not revolve around our desires, hopes, successes, disappointments, and tragedies.

The world moves forward on an unknowable path, guided by the intentions of an all-knowing God. We are privileged to be part of that unfolding of the universe, but we will soon enough leave the part of it we have known. We Christians believe we see only a small part of the known universe here on the earth. I firmly believe there is another universe in another dimension beyond the veil of death.

What comes to your mind when you hear the words, "It's not about you"?

We widow-men have drunk deeply from the fountains of life, love, and learning. We have seen both life and death, and we are in some ways wiser than most of the people around us. Most of us have a few more years to complete our callings on earth. We still have plans and desires to pursue as we move beyond the lives we left behind when our wives died. My prayer for you is that you will be healed of your grief and endowed with the gifts of wisdom and peace as you go from your time of grief to times of joy.

Epilogue

In the opening pages of this book, I recommended that you use this book for your own journaling. In the process of writing it, I found the book serving the purpose of a journal for me too. As I shared my experiences and asked you about yours, I felt my wife's presence more vividly than usual. It was as though she was here, helping me write. I am grateful for what the book has done for me in writing it.

It has been said that death may end a marriage, but it doesn't end the relationship. I'm sure you know, without me telling you, that our hearts and minds are still bonded to our wives even though they are gone. We still see much of life in the light of our experiences with them. Our lives are permanently enriched by the years we shared with our wives, even now as we form new friendships beyond our marriages.

I hope this book has helped deepen your relationship with your departed wife and helped secure many of your precious memories of her through your writing. I hope it has helped prepare you for the next stages of your life. If this book has been helpful, I hope you will consider capturing your experiences, thoughts, and feelings in your own journal in the days and years ahead.

About the Author

Nyle Kardatzke lives in Indianapolis in the home he and his wife bought in 1993. He is retired and spends his time on family, church work, home upkeep, and writing.

Nyle and his wife, Darlene Sayers, married in 1971. They shared life together for thirty-nine years before her death in 2010. Nyle and Darlene have three adult children and nine grandchildren.

Darlene was initially diagnosed with breast cancer in 2003 and went through heavy treatments of chemotherapy followed by a mastectomy, more chemotherapy, and radiation. Through prayer and God's mercy, Darlene was given five more good years. Her cancer returned in March 2009, and she received frequent treatment at the Indiana University Cancer Center until her death on October 25, 2010.

Nyle holds a PhD in economics from UCLA, and he taught economics at Marquette University in Milwaukee before becoming a private school headmaster in 1978. He worked as the Head of School at Brookfield Academy, Wisconsin; Wichita Collegiate School, Kansas; and Sycamore School, Indianapolis; for a total of 28 years before retirement from school headships. Darlene was a pediatrician with a sub-specialty in developmental and behavioral pediatrics. She had a special passion for the mental health of infants and toddlers. A lectureship has been established in her honor at the Indiana University School of Medicine.

Nyle and Darlene were active at the Church at the Crossing in Indianapolis as Sunday school teachers, choir members, and members of the Board of Elders. Nyle has taught a class for senior adults there since 2004.

62207814R00117

Made in the USA
Lexington, KY
31 March 2017